T0063799

101
DEVOTIONS
ON
POWERFUL
PRAYER
for Women

101
DEVOTIONS
ON
POWERFUL
PRAYER
for Women

BARBOUR
PUBLISHING

© 2020 by Barbour Publishing, Inc.

Previously released as *101 Bible Truths for a Powerful Prayer Life*

Editorial assistance by Kayla Coons.

ISBN 978-1-63609-835-7

All rights reserved. No part of this publication may be reproduced or transmitted for commercial purposes, except for brief quotations in printed reviews, without written permission of the publisher. Reproduced text may not be used on the World Wide Web.

Churches and other noncommercial interests may reproduce portions of this book without the express written permission of Barbour Publishing, provided that the text does not exceed 500 words and that the text is not material quoted from another publisher. When reproducing text from this book, include the following credit line: "From *101 Devotions on Powerful Prayer for Women*, published by Barbour Publishing, Inc. Used by permission."

Scripture quotations are taken from the Barbour Simplified KJV, copyright © 2022 by Barbour Publishing, Inc., Uhrichsville, Ohio 44683. All rights reserved.

Cover Design: Greg Jackson, Thinkpen Design

Published by Barbour Publishing, Inc., 1810 Barbour Drive, Uhrichsville, Ohio 44683, www.barbourbooks.com

Our mission is to inspire the world with the life-changing message of the Bible.

ecpa Member of the
Evangelical Christian
Publishers Association

Printed in China.

INTRODUCTION

This book, *101 Devotions on Powerful Prayer for Women*, features devotional readings that unpack scriptural teachings on prayer. We hope they will sink deep into your heart and help you discover the secret of a fulfilling, abundant prayer life.

Many Christians know that prayer is important—essential, really—but still struggle to pray. Biblical commands like "pray without ceasing" (1 Thessalonians 5:17) may sound difficult. . . or even impossible.

And yet, God *wants* to hear from His children. At any time, in any circumstance, we have the privilege of talking with the almighty Creator of the universe. And according to Jesus, the "default setting" of prayer is that His Father will hear and answer: "Ask, and it shall be given to you. Seek, and you shall find. Knock, and it shall be opened to you. For everyone who asks receives, and he who seeks finds, and to him who knocks it shall be opened" (Matthew 7:7–8).

Perhaps that has not been your experience with prayer. Or maybe you've enjoyed success in prayer but would like to be even more effective. Whatever the case, the Bible offers many insights, and this book distills them into 101 principles. They are presented in easy-to-read devotions accompanied by thoughtful "prayer starters."

If you make prayer a priority—by studying its biblical basis and then putting those truths into practice—we're confident that you'll find yourself in a deeper, more intimate relationship with God.

Isn't that what life is all about?

POWERFUL PRAYER
Truth #1

Prayer can be learned.

*And it came to pass, that, as He was praying in a certain
place, when He ceased, one of His disciples said to Him,
"Lord, teach us to pray, as John also taught his disciples."*
LUKE 11:1

We don't know which disciple made this request of Jesus. Nor
do we know *why* he asked for a lesson in prayer. Had he been
frustrated by the process? Did he desire greater results? Was
he unsure of where to begin?

Whatever the case, Jesus seemed happy to give this man and
the other eleven disciples (and *you*) an answer. That answer
contains the first of our 101 Bible truths for a powerful prayer
life: *prayer can be learned*. If that weren't true, the disciple's
request, Jesus' instruction, and the biblical record of them
would be senseless, a spiritual wild-goose chase. God doesn't
work like that.

If you want to pray more powerfully, God will show you how.
Perhaps you know from Hebrews 11:6 "that He is a rewarder
of those who diligently seek Him"—and prayer is part of
both the search and the reward. God wants to lead you into
deeper, more intimate communication with Himself. Your
job is simply to learn.

The Bible will be your guide. As the "word of God," it contains everything you need to know to live successfully in this world. It contains the prayers and prayer examples of great men and women, including Jesus Christ, "the Word" who was in the beginning, who was with God and who is God (John 1:1). What better person could there be to begin our study?

If your desire is more powerful prayer and you're willing to devote some time and energy to it, let's unpack some key Bible truths. We'll start with "the Lord's prayer," Jesus' answer to that unnamed disciple who said, "Teach us to pray."

Can prayer be learned? Absolutely. It must also be practiced. Begin with the following starter prayer, and then spend some time on your own, just talking with your heavenly Father.

Lord God, like Jesus' disciples, I want to learn how to pray. I ask You to guide me into a deeper, more intimate communion, based on the truth of Your Word. Please give me insight, focus, and stamina as I learn this important skill. In Jesus' name, I pray, amen.

POWERFUL PRAYER
Truth #2

Prayer is talking with our Father.

"When you pray, say: Our Father who is in heaven, Hallowed be Your name."

LUKE 11:2

You probably wouldn't call your dad the "benevolent dictator" or "male head of household." You likely have a more intimate name, like *dad*, *pa*, or *father*. Jesus thought it important to call God His own Father—but He took that idea a step beyond by including all of us. Jesus taught Christians to say, *"Our* Father who is in heaven."

Fathers are always older and often wiser than their children. So, prayer to God is your all-access pass to learning from one who knows more, has experienced more, and loves more than you do.

You're not talking to someone who's impersonal and out of touch. You're not talking to someone who's quick to point out your faults and remind you of the mess you've made. You're not begging a judge for a plea bargain to try to escape the trouble you face.

No, you get to talk to the one who's fully aware that you've fallen short of His glory again (see Romans 3:23) but offers forgiveness anyway. Then it's like He offers a warm, fatherly hug: "Blessed be God, even the Father of our Lord Jesus Christ, the Father of mercies and the God of all comfort, who comforts us in all our tribulation, that we may be able to comfort those who are in any trouble, by the comfort with which we ourselves are comforted by God" (2 Corinthians 1:3–4). He can (and will) restore your relationship with Him.

When you understand how much God does for you, it might be hard to think of Him as your "cosmic buddy" or "the man upstairs." He should be honored because He will always do more for you than anyone else possibly could. He's your Father—*and He loves you.*

Lord God, it's comforting to know I can call You "Father." Thanks for the reminder that You never see me as someone who is unworthy of a close relationship. Help me remember that no matter how I feel about myself, You love me. Amen.

POWERFUL PRAYER
Truth #3

Prayer aligns your will with God's.

"When you pray, say. . . . Your kingdom come.
Your will be done, as in heaven, so on earth."

LUKE 11:2

It's not uncommon for us to compartmentalize our lives. We act one way in church and another at home. The way we act at work may be different than when we're around a certain set of friends.

The apostle Peter wrote, "but as He who has called you is holy, so you be holy in all manner of conduct, because it is written, 'Be holy, for I am holy' " (1 Peter 1:15–16). If you reread that carefully, you'll see that because God is holy (set apart for a good purpose), you should also be set apart because He called you to be different. This includes every part of your life, not just time for a church service on the weekend.

This part of Jesus' model prayer is a reminder that His kingdom has a delivery date and that His will ultimately will be done, everywhere. Jesus didn't compartmentalize anything, and Hebrews 13:8 puts an exclamation point on this by saying, "Jesus Christ is the same yesterday, and today, and forever." *He never changes.*

Jesus' belief and behavior didn't change based on world events, opinion polls, or popularity contests. Neither should ours. Embrace His example and remain a true child of God at church, at home, at work, or with any friend you can name.

We should want what God wants, do what God does, and love like He loves. Don't find yourself in a fight against God—you can't win. (You can't even tie or break even.)

So, pray with an unpacked heart, without any compartment that reads OFF LIMITS. Invite God's will to be demonstrated in a holy, set-aside life. This isn't a call to pride, just for Christians to live up to their name. It's a call that comes from a changeless God.

Dear God, the things that You have planned for our world will happen. You want me to agree that Your plan is best and allow it to change my world. May I cooperate with Your plan, so it never even looks like I'm fighting against You. Amen.

POWERFUL PRAYER
Truth #4

Prayer is asking God to meet our needs.

"Give us day by day our daily bread."
LUKE 11:3

This short sentence, tucked inside the greatest prayer known to humankind, doesn't ask for a daily four-course meal. Jesus didn't suggest you request special dishes from a short list of favorites. God will meet our needs, but He rarely caters to demands.

Jesus didn't even suggest you make this request personal. The verse is clear: "Give us day by day our daily bread." Did you notice the words *us* and *our*? Praying for the needs of others is an important aspect of praying for our own needs. We shouldn't make prayer exclusive to our personal experience but *inclusive* by sharing the needs of all humanity—even those we might think cruel, those who wear the nametag ENEMY.

You've probably read Luke 11:3 many times. Even when we see the pronouns *us* and *our*, many of us think in terms of what God can do for us personally. Of course, God's answers to prayer can be very personal, but this verse seeks to ward off selfishness in the process. If God is personally invested in answering your prayer, then you can be personally invested in caring about the needs of others. If you think this seems like a new idea, consider Proverbs 21:13: "Whoever stops his ears at the cry of the poor, he also shall cry himself, but shall not be heard."

God cares about every human being. And He wants *you* to care about every human being. Pray for them and help them whenever you can. The prayer you pray for daily bread connects you to the God who provides—and to the people He loves.

Lord, I've been guilty of emphasizing my own needs and assuming You'd take care of the rest without my personal involvement. Maybe I have been missing the point: my needs are no more important than the needs of others—and You love us all. Amen.

POWERFUL PRAYER
Truth #5

Prayer is a tale of two forgivenesses.

*"And forgive us our sins, for we also forgive
everyone who is indebted to us."*

LUKE 11:4

The Lord's prayer continues to invite you to pray for others
while you pray for yourself. But Jesus' teaching doesn't stop
with generalities. More than saying God should forgive the
sins of humankind, this verse indicates that *we* need to do
what we want *Him* to do: forgive.

It's easy to think that when people have hurt us badly, they
don't deserve to be forgiven. We might even be tempted to
place conditions on forgiveness. Sure, maybe we'd consider
forgiving others if they made amends, but how much effort
on their part would be enough? Or maybe we would consider
forgiving people if only they asked, but sometimes they just
don't care.

If you think this prayer of Jesus is a mistake, look at 1 John
1:9: "If we confess our sins, He is faithful and just to forgive us
our sins and to cleanse us from all unrighteousness."

That takes care of the first part of Luke 11:4, but what about
the second? That's in Mark 11:25: "And when you stand praying,
forgive, if you have anything against anyone, that your Father
who is in heaven may also forgive you for your trespasses."

God wants you to act like Him. If He's willing to forgive the "God laws" you break, then it should be a small thing to forgive others when they offend you—whether they know of their offense or not.

You don't have to embrace anger, bitterness, and long-term pain when you've been offended. Move other people out of your personal penalty box and get on with the business of following God.

A lack of forgiveness hurts your relationship with God and other people. He made you to relate to others—and unforgiveness builds walls where bridges should be.

Lord, there are times when I'm happy to be forgiven, but I don't want to forgive. It's like reviewing a car accident over and over again: it doesn't solve the pain, and it adds to my tension. Forgive me, Father. Help me forgive others and heal me. Amen.

POWERFUL PRAYER
Truth #6

Prayer is a request for protection.

*"And do not lead us into temptation,
but deliver us from evil."*

Luke 11:4

This part of the Lord's prayer would have meant something to Job. If you remember his story, you'll recall that everything that could go wrong did. God allowed Satan to take away Job's property, family, and health, all to prove that this man would be faithful.

The word *temptation* in this verse may also be translated as "trials." Trials can lead to a temptation to be faithless—and that's something we should want to be delivered from.

The apostle Paul wrote, "No temptation has taken you but such as is common to man. But God is faithful, who will not allow you to be tempted above what you are able, but with the temptation will also make a way of escape, that you may be able to bear it" (1 Corinthians 10:13).

Whether you face temptations or trials, God can lead you in a better direction: *away from evil*. Learn from trials, accept God's help when you're tempted, and then, "Submit yourselves, therefore, to God. Resist the devil and he will flee from you" (James 4:7).

Think of any characters of the Bible, and you'll see that they faced either trials or temptations. With God's help, some made it through the struggle—people like Joseph, Abraham, Esther, and Daniel. Others, such as David, Samson, and Jonah, didn't take God's help at key points in life and encountered struggles that followed them for years.

Of course, no one but Jesus made perfect choices all the time. The examples of other Bible characters were captured so we could see the good and bad associated with trials and temptation. You'll see the best by praying for and accepting God's help.

Dear God, sin seems to follow me all the days of my life—but so does Your goodness and mercy. Hard days come and some even lead to the valley of the shadow of death. Remind me of Your wisdom and keep me from walking by myself. Amen.

POWERFUL PRAYER
Truth #7

Prayer is acknowledging God's goodness and power.

"For Yours is the kingdom and the power and the glory forever."

Matthew 6:13

Build the most powerful engine humankind has ever seen and there will come a day when that engine stops working. Research any kingdom—there is always a rise and a fall. Think of humanity's heroes, and you'll discover their glory fades over time. *Not so with God.*

How important is God's kingdom? Well, Jesus said you should make finding it a priority: "But seek first the kingdom of God and His righteousness" (Matthew 6:33).

God's kingdom didn't originate on earth (see John 18:36). It includes righteousness, peace, and joy (Romans 14:17). It was introduced by Jesus (Matthew 4:17). Not everyone qualifies for this kingdom (see Galatians 5:19–21 and John 3:3). No other kingdom will ever be more important than God's (Psalm 103:19).

When it comes to God's *power*, 1 Chronicles 29:11 declares, "Yours, O Lord, is the greatness and the power and the glory and the victory and the majesty, for all that is in heaven and on the earth is Yours. Yours is the kingdom, O Lord, and You are exalted as head above all."

And Isaiah 42:8 puts God's *glory* into perspective: "I am the LORD—that is My name—and I will not give My glory to another or My praise to carved images."

These are snapshots of what it looks like to pray, "For Yours is the kingdom and the power and the glory forever."

For seven days now, we've taken a closer look at the Lord's Prayer. And this prayer journey has just begun. A preview of coming attractions includes instructions from biblical prayers and lessons about prayer, drawn from both the Old and New Testaments. There's encouragement with each turn of the page. Before you continue, why not offer a quick prayer of thanks to God?

---

*Lord, I don't want to give glory to anything
besides You. I don't want to believe that anything
could be more powerful than You or settle for
a kingdom less worthy than Yours. I honor
and acknowledge Your greatness. Amen.*

POWERFUL PRAYER
Truth #8

Prayer blesses others.

*"The LORD bless you and keep you. The LORD make His
face shine on you and be gracious to you. The LORD
lift up His countenance on you and give you peace."*

NUMBERS 6:24–26

The past seven days have been dedicated to Jesus' model prayer
for His disciples. Today we'll look at "God's prayer" given to
Moses' brother, Aaron.

Aaron needed to understand that God wanted to bless His
people. And the blessings He spoke about in this prayer have
very little to do with money or possessions. The apostle Paul
put a fine edge on defining God's blessing when he wrote,
"Christ has redeemed us from the curse of the law, being
made a curse for us—for it is written, 'Cursed is everyone who
hangs on a tree'—that the blessing of Abraham might come
on the Gentiles through Jesus Christ, that we might receive
the promise of the Spirit through faith" (Galatians 3:13–14).

Jesus became your greatest blessing. Faith in Him preserves
(or "keeps") you. God can make His face shine upon you when
you accept His Son. He's gracious to you because you're part
of His family. He can lift up His countenance to you because
He's always wanted a relationship with you. His peace can be
yours because you embraced His blessings. Jesus came for all

humankind, taking your punishment and replacing it with a blessing.

When you pray, you should want the best for the people you bring before God. How would things change if you prayed God's prayer for family, friends, and even enemies?

If you struggle to pray this prayer, consider what it would mean to pray a prayer of opposites: "The Lord curse you, and keep you at arm's length; the Lord hide His face from you, and be cruel to you; the Lord find you unacceptable and leave you without peace."

Could you really pray that? God gave us a great example, a better choice—a better prayer.

Father God, Your model prayer tells so much about You. There's a love and grace in these words that should change me and change the way I pray. Through Jesus, every part of this prayer becomes a practical way for me to bless others in my time with You. Amen.

POWERFUL PRAYER
Truth #9

Prayer can bring dread.

*[Adam] said, "I heard Your voice in
the garden, and I was afraid."*
GENESIS 3:10

If prayer is defined as a conversation with God, then Genesis 3:10 is the very first prayer recorded in the Bible. You might expect the first prayer to be majestic, honorable, and filled with worship. But that wasn't the case.

The first man and woman were given one command. The fruit of one tree in the garden was off-limits. Adam blamed Eve, since she took the first bite; Eve blamed the serpent, since he had tempted her; and the couple even tried to blame God for the situation. As Genesis 3:12 reads, "The man said, 'The woman *whom You gave to be with me*, she gave me from the tree, and I ate' " (emphasis added).

The first humans' conversation with God led to dread because they had to admit that *they* had broken the only command God gave. Adam delivered his "prayer" with an equal mixture of blame and defiance rather than sorrow and repentance.

It may be worth considering the similar first voice-to-voice conversation between Job and God. Job had lost everything, and he wanted to know why. After allowing Job to complain at length, God replied. And when Job heard what God had to say, he responded, "Behold, I am vile. What shall I answer You? I will lay my hand on my mouth. Once I have spoken, but I will not answer—yes, twice, but I will proceed no further" (Job 40:4–5).

Job had a very different perspective than Adam and Eve. He recognized the majesty and the glory of God—and instead of being defiant, Job displayed humility and awe. That would have served Adam and Eve well. It would look good on you too.

Lord, I want to be honest when I blow it. Help me never to blame others for my choice to disobey. And when I read a response from Your Word, help me to accept it with humility and awe. May prayer be a key part of my relationship with You. Amen.

POWERFUL PRAYER
Truth #10

Prayer shouldn't be for show.

*"But you, when you pray, enter into your closet,
and when you have shut your door, pray to your
Father who is in secret. And your Father who
sees in secret shall reward you openly."*

MATTHEW 6:6

Prayer is a private conversation between children of God and their Father. It's not a performance, a sermon in disguise, or a way to show others how spiritual you are. We pray to an audience of one even when others may overhear.

Jesus condemned a Pharisee who prayed, "God, I thank You that I am not as other men are—extortioners, unjust, adulterers, or even as this tax collector" (Luke 18:11). This prayer did not impress God, who wants His children to seek and know Him as they are sought and known by Him. As the apostle Peter wrote, "Since you have purified your souls in obeying the truth through the Spirit in sincere love of the brothers, see that you love one another fervently with a pure heart" (1 Peter 1:22).

Prayer isn't the end of a spiritual talent show. It's the overflow of a sinner saved by grace, who's intentional about saying thanks. Prayer comes from the heart of a questioner who really wants to know what God thinks. Prayer voices concern by one sinner for another. It's praise, worship, and wonder.

Jesus prayed in front of people, but there were times when He needed to just get away. Luke 5:16 says, "He withdrew Himself into the wilderness and prayed."

Praying in public shouldn't be more thrilling than a prayer offered in the middle of the night when anxiety wrestles with your sleep. It shouldn't be something you seek more than a tender God-greeting at the start of a difficult day. It shouldn't be the pursuit of even one human "atta boy." Prayer is turning to God because you need to talk.

Dear God, may my search for approval end with Your acceptance. Help me use prayer to learn more about Your plans for me, not as a way to feel more significant around other people. Remind me that I'll never find a greater listener than You. Amen.

POWERFUL PRAYER
Truth #11

Prayer admits that God is incomparable.

There is no one holy like the LORD, for there is no one besides You, nor is there any rock like our God.

1 SAMUEL 2:2

Human beings like to compare. We compare things, and we compare ourselves to other people—what we look like, how much money we make, what our accomplishments are, and so on. We might even try comparing ourselves to God.

But God has no peer. In Isaiah 55:8, God says, "For My thoughts are not your thoughts, nor are your ways My ways." God is without equal and is perfect. No one is wiser, stronger, or holier.

There's no sane comparison between *any* person and God. And you can take that a step further: "Among the gods there is none like You, O Lord" (Psalm 86:8). If you're looking for an apples-to-apples comparison for God, it's not possible. He is *incomparable*.

Your prayers should reflect that truth. God is not like you. He never breaks His law (2 Timothy 2:13). His truth is absolute and yours cannot always be trusted (John 1:14). He chose to love you while you chose rebellion (Romans 5:8).

Compare yourself any way you want and you'll be found lacking. Paul wrote, "For all have sinned and come short of the glory of God" (Romans 3:23). This kind of comparison might be a little like telling the God who created the Grand Canyon that you will prove your worth by jumping the width of the canyon. It can't be done and it's foolish to try.

In prayer, admit that God is incomparable.

Father, You're a big God with big plans and a perfect track record. You're worth following because there's no one better. Your faithfulness is flawless. Your truth? Absolute. Where You lead, let me follow. May I gain perspective when I compare my imperfect self to Your perfection. Amen.

POWERFUL PRAYER
Truth #12

Prayer is an act of devotion.

*"But we will give ourselves continually to
prayer and to the ministry of the word."*

ACTS 6:4

We're often told to work hard for the things we want. But while
pursuing our wants, we can lose communication with God.

There's an old hymn that says, "This world is not my home,
I'm just a passin' through." It's become too easy to set aside the
pursuit of heaven in favor of earthly pleasures. God has made
sharing His love a prime directive, but sometimes personal
interests replace the giving of ourselves continually to prayer.
We allow God's Word to sit neglected.

Prayer is a never-failing open line to God but can be set aside
and seemingly abandoned. God's Word contains answers for
living but has become a part of home décor. It might even be
placed in a holding cell in a closet or drawer for an undeter-
mined future reference.

Is the work you were given to do by God sitting idle? Have
the things of this world replaced prayer and God's Word in
importance?

The first-century church admitted that ongoing communication was important to their ministry. Talking to God and
learning from Him were the most important things they could

do—and they *seemed* committed to doing just that. Being sidetracked didn't fit into the purpose they'd been given. So they were right to make this bold declaration, and it's a fitting challenge today, but they failed from time to time. They got distracted, and they needed reminders of their purpose. They needed forgiveness.

Prayer and Bible reading aren't exercises in which you learn facts and then share *what* you know instead of *Who* you know. Think relationship. Mutual devotion between God and you is worth more than anything on earth and offers an eternal transport to the place where God lives.

Lord God, You have answers for life. I want to keep the lines of communication open between You and me. I want Your Word to impact my choices. I want prayer to keep my focus on You. May I learn Your purpose for me and seek time with You. Amen.

POWERFUL PRAYER
Truth #13

Prayer is commitment.

But I will sacrifice to You with the voice of thanksgiving.
I will pay what I have vowed. Salvation is of the LORD.

JONAH 2:9

If God has ever given you an attitude adjustment, then you can probably identify with the prophet Jonah. He needed one.

God asked Jonah to deliver a message to the people of Nineveh. It was a simple message: "Repent." It seemed an easy request. People *should* be made aware that God wants them to turn their backs on sin. All Jonah had to do was deliver the message. He wasn't responsible for making the people obey, he didn't need to personally approve of the content of the message, and it wouldn't take him long to do what God asked. Jonah just didn't want to do it.

Jonah was not a fan of the people of Nineveh. He would have been happy to see the people destroyed. So the prophet made a mad dash on a big ship headed the wrong way—on purpose. God was not amused.

God sent a big fish, and Jonah found himself in the fish's belly, facing a three-day time-out. The verse above was the last prayer Jonah would pray from inside the fish. In the very next verse, Jonah is set back on track once he came around to God's way of thinking: "And the LORD spoke to the fish, and it vomited out Jonah on the dry land" (Jonah 2:10).

God wanted a message delivered and Jonah delivered it—after a short detour. Sometimes the trouble you face is exactly what you need to get you to the place where you can show gratitude to a God who gave you a purpose and instructions to follow. God rescues. He saves. He is committed to His family. Jonah began to understand that he needed to be committed to God's plan.

God, I don't want to be as stubborn as Jonah, but I probably will be. Transform my good intentions into a commitment that leads to obedience. When I know the right thing to do, help me do it without delay. I don't want to run from Your plan. Amen.

POWERFUL PRAYER
Truth #14

Prayer can bring about healing.

Confess your faults to one another and pray for one another, that you may be healed. The effective fervent prayer of a righteous man avails much.

JAMES 5:16

Two words that have been used to describe how Christians should respond to other Christians are *authentic* and *transparent*. That means if you haven't followed God very well, you shouldn't lie about it. If you face a struggle, you should feel free to share it with believers who will pray for you.

Sometimes Christians who fail have felt that sharing their faults would result in being shunned by other Christians—Christians who also sin. Today's verse clearly states that confessing sin and praying for others can bring healing. This can mean spiritual, emotional, and perhaps physical healing. A practical reason for physical healing is the reduction in anxiety. Without anxiety, physical health improves.

People who love God and love His people pray for each other and can expect good things—whatever God sends in answer to the prayers, even if it's not what we immediately desire. When Christians belittle each other and compare themselves, there's little authenticity, transparency, or healing.

God's idea for relationship goes beyond a connection

between Himself and individual people. He wants strong relationships for biological families. He wants strong relationships for His spiritual family too. Sadly, there are many instances when people who should be authentic and transparent put on a mask. Sometimes we wear masks because we don't trust fellow Christians; other times we struggle to admit we're wounded or wonder what people will think. But when you wear a mask, seeking to hide faults, scars, and pain, you're avoiding the remedy God put in place to bring healing to His people.

Give others a reason to trust you, and then pray for each other. Bring on the healing.

Father God, You forgive, but I struggle to share everything with You. Sometimes people struggle to forgive, so it's easy to go into hiding rather than share my heart with other Christians. I long for the comfort of being authentic and transparent with You and Your people. Amen.

POWERFUL PRAYER
Truth #15

Prayer gets God's attention.

Hear my prayer, O LORD, give ear to my
supplications; in Your faithfulness answer
me, and in Your righteousness.

PSALM 143:1

It should seem obvious that when you pray, God listens. Maybe it's so obvious you wonder why it's worth discussing. After all, you understand the connection between prayer and a conversation with God. But there's much more to this declaration.

When you pray, you're talking to God. Let that sink in for a moment. This isn't a call to a customer service department, a call to a good friend, or a call to your favorite restaurant. You're talking to God, and His full attention is on you. The psalmist wrote, "Keep me as the apple of the eye. Hide me under the shadow of Your wings" (Psalm 17:8). God is concerned with the things that concern you. He loves you. Prayer gets God's attention because you've chosen to talk to Him, and we can be sure that He listens, He's faithful to answer, and He's completely righteous.

Even so, it's a good thing to enter any time of prayer with respect and honor. The idea of God as a pal fails to take into account who He is and minimizes His gift of listening to you. The psalmist didn't want anything to hinder his prayer, including his attitude. He begs God to listen, lets God know he needs help, and requests that, because God is faithful and righteous, He would answer his prayer.

Make no mistake, God listens even when you don't come to Him with a sense of awe—but people of the Bible considered their time with God a serious privilege, not an afterthought. They were fully engaged in their prayer when they sought His answer.

Lord, may my time with You be precious to both of us. I want this time to be well spent and honorable to You. I don't want to waste Your time by making this conversation with You seem unimportant. You are so gracious to listen and let me speak. Amen.

POWERFUL PRAYER
Truth #16

Prayers are uttered by the imperfect.

And do not enter into judgment with Your servant,
for in Your sight no man living shall be justified.

PSALM 143:2

You'll never surprise God by admitting you're imperfect. It won't shock Him or come as unexpected news. He knows you're imperfect. Admitting your sin to Him is actually a much better response than offering excuses, blaming someone else, or saying it's not true.

King David pleaded for mercy even though sin demands justice. If he were perfect, there would be no reason for mercy. But David knew that if God judged him based on his ability to follow His law, then he'd never be justified or have a clear account with God. The truth is, if God didn't show mercy, no one could live to tell of His goodness.

David described himself as a servant who fails. He recognized that God's eyesight is perfect. He sees everything and knows what we'd rather keep hidden.

It might appear that God is out to discover everything He possibly can in order to find fault. Hopefully, you're learning that God is aware of your imperfections and still wants to connect with you. The psalmist's words should encourage you: "Enter into His gates with thanksgiving and into His courts with praise; be thankful to Him, and bless His name. For the LORD is good; His mercy is everlasting, and His truth endures to all generations" (Psalm 100:4–5).

The mercy and grace you need come from the same God who has every right to condemn you. And the good news continues: "Therefore there is now no condemnation for those who are in Christ Jesus, who walk according to the Spirit, not according to the flesh" (Romans 8:1). Jesus paid the full price for your sin. Walk and talk with God; *mercy* is His preference.

Jesus said it best in John 8:11: "Go and sin no more."

Father God, if I waited until I was perfect to pray, then I couldn't talk to You. Much of my life involves making choices—and either believing I've made a good choice or regretting another failure. You want me to admit my imperfections and seek Your help. Amen.

POWERFUL PRAYER
Truth #17

Prayers are uttered by the struggler.

For the enemy has persecuted my soul; he has struck
my life down to the ground; he has made me to dwell
in darkness, like those who have been long dead.
PSALM 143:3

You have an enemy—and it's not God. You're at war—and God is the commander. You have armor—and every piece is for defense.

This miniseries continues in Psalm 143. The struggle has become very real for King David, who admits he's been persecuted, crushed, subjected to darkness, and left for dead. David's bold declaration follows an admission of imperfection. He needs direction from the commander-in-chief. Help is on the way.

Maybe you've been there. Bad days accumulate faster than Frequent Flyer miles. Uncertainty chases every decision you make. You hear whispers saying God couldn't love you, and you're beginning to believe it. You're battle weary and convinced you don't belong on the front lines. It all seems. . .too much.

In this place of struggle, there's encouragement. Paul told the Corinthians, "Watch, stand fast in the faith, act like men, be strong" (1 Corinthians 16:13). When you want to give up— stand fast. When you're weary—stand fast. When you want a new assignment—stand fast.

God knows your struggle, and He walks with you in each trial you face. He doesn't leave you defenseless. Any strength you have comes from Him. Paul wrote, "Finally, my brothers, be strong in the Lord and in the power of His might" (Ephesians 6:10). (When you have time, check out the full armor of God in Ephesians 6:11–18, because "we wrestle not against flesh and blood but against principalities, against powers, against the rulers of the darkness of this world, against spiritual wickedness in high places" [verse 12].)

Struggle, knowing you never struggle alone. Struggle, knowing you stand in the strength of God. Struggle, knowing there will come a day when all struggles will be over. Embrace grace for today, hope for tomorrow, and peace in the meantime, knowing God is with you now—and always.

Dear Lord, my struggle makes me want to give up.
The trials I face wear me down. I've tried to manage
without help and I can't. I've wanted to quit, and You tell
me to stand. I'm a struggler because all people struggle.
I'm an overcomer because You overcame. Amen.

POWERFUL PRAYER
Truth #18

Prayers are uttered by the overwhelmed.

*Therefore my spirit is overwhelmed within
me; my heart is desolate within me.*
PSALM 143:4

In Psalm 143:4, David moved beyond weariness, beyond the struggle, and beyond acknowledging imperfection. He was in a place where he doubted what he knew and had no strength to move forward.

When you utter a "prayer of the overwhelmed," you're at the lowest points in life. If life is a rubber band, it's snapped; if it's a balloon, it's popped; and if it's a river, it's flooded. Everything that could go wrong has. You haven't taken the time to think about any better days that may arrive in the future. It's too much work to think about good things in the past. This is a place of pain, and survival has dominated your thoughts.

Many who find themselves in this place sink into escapism. If they can find something that compensates for the pain, they take it, drink it, or try it. But there's a better way.

David admitted he was overwhelmed. He was honest in saying that he felt desolate. He came to the end of his rope and wasn't sure where to turn. This was the worst day among many bad days for King David, but the downward spiral was about to end. Rescue would come. "Those who wait on the

LORD shall renew their strength. They shall mount up with wings like eagles, they shall run and not be weary, and they shall walk and not faint" (Isaiah 40:31).

Without the storms of the overwhelmed, there would be no stories of God's faithfulness. People will need the encouragement of the overwhelmed because they will need the hope that the dark night they face will lead to a better day.

Be honest when you pray. If you're overwhelmed, tell God, and let Him lead you out.

Lord, if I'm not overwhelmed right now, I have been and will be again. Because You bring me through pain, help me encourage others who are where I've been. I want to be honest when I talk to You. When I'm overwhelmed, help me admit it and accept Your help. Amen.

POWERFUL PRAYER
Truth #19

Prayers are uttered by those who remember.

*I remember the days of old; I meditate on all Your
works; I muse on the work of Your hands.*

PSALM 143:5

This is for all the down-and-outers, the completely over-whelmed, the strugglers. This is for those who are gripping pain, hiding hurt, shedding tears, and dreading sleepless nights.

Why? This is a pivot point from pain to purpose, tears to triumph, and hurt to healing. It's the dawning of a new day. It's the recognition that "this is the day that the LORD has made; we will rejoice and be glad in it" (Psalm 118:24).

It may sound too simple, but the path that leads away from Overwhelmed On-Ramp is a side trip down Memory Lane. This isn't reliving personal glory days but remembering God's glory. It isn't a recounting of awards and achievements but remembering God's goodness and grace. It won't be counting net worth and property values but a complete review of God's plan, purpose, and provision.

Sometimes this process is called "counting blessings." Your hardest life obstacles are no problem for a God who makes Goliath grasshoppers, ring-tailed lemurs, and perfect sunsets. Your personal creativity can't begin to imagine all the beauty

God has created. The sacrifices you've made are infinitely smaller than the sacrifice of God's Son, who can save you from your own dark days.

Think about what God has made. Think about what He's done. Think about His love for you. "Remember the former things of old," God said in Isaiah 46:9, "for I am God, and there is no one else. I am God, and there is no one like Me."

Make remembering personal. What has God done *for you*? Where have you seen God's footprints? When have you followed those prints? How has God answered your prayers? What are some things only God can do?

Remember. Muse. Meditate.

Father, I want better days, and I'm tired of trying to make it happen on my own. Take my worry and transform it into worship. Take my bad days and make them blessings. Take my heart and make it healthy. When I talk to You, I'm not so overwhelmed. Amen.

POWERFUL PRAYER
Truth #20

Prayers are uttered by those who need more of God.

I stretch out my hands to You; my soul
thirsts for You, like a thirsty land.

PSALM 143:6

The overwhelmed need God. The strugglers need God. The down-and-outers need God. Chances are, you've been all three, which means *you* need God.

The psalmist said, "As the deer pants for the water brooks, so my soul pants for You, O God. My soul thirsts for God, for the living God" (Psalm 42:1–2). This kind of longing isn't just a willingness to add God to your arsenal of hope. God becomes *everything* to you. He's as essential as air, as needed as water, and as vital as daily bread. Your prayers should make it clear that you're not just dipping your toe in Christianity; you're all in—and you'll go to the deep end because God's the lifeguard.

Closeness with God becomes more tangible when you remember the trenches He's rescued you from, when you recall painful days that were met with His grace and mercy, and when you're certain there's no personal drought God can't fix with a flood of faithfulness.

The good news? God has always been reaching toward you. The question you must wrestle with is how willing you are to reach out to Him. If you're like many Christians, you try to save God some time and effort by trying to manage life on your own. You've made God your emergency contact should all else fail.

God doesn't want to be thought of as a remote figure in the head office. If He met you in the trenches, then He can walk with you in your everyday life. Not by remote, not only when He believes you're worthy, and not just when you extend an invitation.

Stretch your spiritual hands in God's direction, admit your thirst for God's help, and always accept it when it arrives at just the right time.

Dear God, as removed from life as I feel when I'm overwhelmed, help me feel as connected to You when I remember Your faithfulness and acknowledge how much I need You. This is a prayer of dependency on You. Help me—because I need Your help. Amen.

POWERFUL PRAYER
Truth #21

Prayers are uttered by the lonely.

Hear me speedily, O LORD. My spirit fails; do not hide Your face from me, lest I be like those who go down into the pit.

PSALM 143:7

You can live with a houseful of people and still feel lonely. It's not a matter of how many people are around, but how connected you feel. When isolated by choice or circumstance, you feel lonely. That's when you need to pray.

King David felt a heavy sense of loneliness. He prayed for quick connection with God. David wondered how his life was any different from those who "go down into the pit."

Over the past several days, you've been reading various aspects of this prayer, and it's full of raw emotion. David seems to remember the urgency of his prayer and returns to expressing his need for help. If this sounds conflicted or even scattered, it's good to remember that we're encouraged to pray authentic prayers. Read David's prayer again. At one moment, David speaks the words of a wounded heart, but soon, words of worship and wonder make a debut. Have you ever prayed that kind of prayer? Has a broken heart fully expressed to the Great Healer resulted in the transformation of loneliness and loss to love and life?

Feelings like loneliness show our humanity. Loneliness is a

malady common to all humankind. While you can agree that as a Christ follower you're never really alone, you'd be hard-pressed to convince your heart. Still, *God is always with you.* Believe it even when you don't feel like it's true.

Need more convincing? God says in Isaiah 41:10, "Do not fear, for I am with you. Do not be dismayed, for I am your God. I will strengthen you. Yes, I will help you. Yes, I will uphold you with My righteous right hand."

---

*Father, my greatest relationship is with You,
but sometimes I feel so alone. I want to know You,
but sometimes it feels as if too much time has passed
since we first met. Have we grown apart? Make Yourself
known to me. Show Your love to me once more. Amen.*

POWERFUL PRAYER
Truth #22

Prayers are uttered by those seeking direction.

Cause me to hear Your loving-kindness in the morning,
for in You I trust. Cause me to know the way in
which I should walk, for I lift up my soul to You.

PSALM 143:8

David didn't say he trusted people or even his own opinion or decision-making skills. *David trusted God.* When he woke up, he wanted to be reminded of God's loving-kindness. His day needed to start with consistent "God reminders."

If you've ever wondered how important God really is, consider the depths of discouragement that King David faced. The king wanted a close friendship with God. Why? Psalm 23 provides a great answer. "Yes, though I walk through the valley of the shadow of death, I will not fear evil, for You are with me. Your rod and Your staff, they comfort me. You prepare a table before me in the presence of my enemies. You anoint my head with oil. My cup runs over. Surely goodness and mercy shall follow me all the days of my life, and I will dwell in the house of the LORD forever" (verses 4–6).

God is more than a glorified spiritual road map. His leadership is personal, and He never gets lost. Feel free to pray the prayer of the directionally challenged. You're human—you'll need direction.

It can be easy to seek out self-help when you need God's help. It's easy to determine a direction without asking the divine. It's easy, but not productive.

Join David in a desperate prayer that says, "Cause me to know the way in which I should walk." If this prayer isn't in your heart and on your lips, you're stumbling in the dark, making your best guess, and getting off track.

David realized the fragile nature of getting lost; he'd been lost before. In a very vulnerable moment, he prayed, "I lift up my soul to You." He appealed to God's compassion to restore spiritual health and care for his very soul.

Lord, I can set goals, but I really don't know where I'm going. You do. Guide me in the way You want me to go. Give guidance to my goals and help in my decision-making. You have the directions I need. May I always ask for Your help. Amen.

POWERFUL PRAYER
Truth #23

Prayers are uttered by those seeking deliverance.

Deliver me, O LORD, from my enemies.
I flee to You to hide me.
PSALM 143:9

King David faced real enemies that sought to end his life. He needed deliverance, and God was on speed dial. David's prayer in Psalm 143 was desperate, urgent, and specific. If God didn't show up, there was no plan B.

You have enemies too. They might not threaten you physically, but they're opposed to what you stand for and believe in. Sometimes you can even become your own worst enemy through the choices you make.

A good reminder for all of us is found in Deuteronomy 31:6—"Be strong and of good courage. Do not fear or be afraid of them, for the LORD your God, it is He who goes with you. He will not fail you or forsake you."

Isn't it encouraging that in virtually all instances of prayer in the Bible, there are verses that deal with how God takes care of that kind of prayer? For each of the 101 scripture selections in this book, you'll discover that God not only is on the job but also has the answers, a willingness to help, and an incredible purpose for you.

Think of a time when you were desperate for deliverance. You did your best to figure out a way to rescue yourself before you ever prayed for God's help. Humans do that. You might think you're just following the adage "God helps those who help themselves." The trouble is that statement isn't in the Bible. Psalm 143:9 clashes with the idea when Israel's most famous king asked for deliverance instead. David put it well: "Some trust in chariots and some in horses, but we will remember the name of the LORD our God" (Psalm 20:7).

Father God, I admit there are times when I accept ideas as coming from You when they aren't in Your Word. Help me to ask for help and seek Your answers in the words You wrote for me and for my good. Deliver me and keep me out of Your way. Amen.

POWERFUL PRAYER
Truth #24

Prayers are uttered by those willing to learn.

*Teach me to do Your will, for You are my God. Your
Spirit is good; lead me into the land of uprightness.*

PSALM 143:10

Sometimes you can be your own worst enemy. King David
admitted his willingness to learn, but he'd rather learn from
the best than live with a wealth of personal life experience.

Think about how much time you'd save if you could just
accept God's instruction as the right answer instead of a suggestion to consider. God has a plan for you. Do you really *want*
to know what it is? You could just make your own choices and
find a life plan that appeals to you. But consider a few biblical
examples. Peter was content to be a fisherman, but God had
other plans. Ruth could have stayed in her home country
instead of going with Naomi who was following God—who had
other plans for them. Zacchaeus was happy collecting more tax
than he should, but God—you guessed it!—*had other plans*.

Each one was directed to God's own plan, and it changed their
lives. God said in Psalm 32:8, "I will instruct you and teach you
in the way that you shall go." This doesn't sound like a God who
couldn't care less about what you do. It doesn't even sound like
He's willing to cancel class because you've been tardy too many
times. He has a great plan for your life, and He's interested in

knowing if you're willing to learn. So pray—and let Him know you're ready.

God is the only one who can provide the perfect instruction you need to lead you "into the land of uprightness." Don't settle for the Land of the Morally Superior, the Island of Advanced Biblical Facts, or the Straits of Spiritual Mediocrity. God is giving free lessons, and the lessons you accept now are much more enjoyable than those taught after skipping God's class.

Lord, You're my Teacher, and I'm guilty of being tardy, inattentive, or completely absent. Help me discover value in Your lessons. I want to know You, follow You, and learn from You. I can't do that when I refuse to open Your instruction book. Give me the desire to learn. Amen.

POWERFUL PRAYER
Truth #25

Prayers are uttered by those who recognize trouble.

Revive me, O LORD, for Your name's sake; for Your righteousness' sake bring my soul out of trouble.

PSALM 143:11

This prayer verse boldly recognizes that trouble has crash-landed. This could be the trouble delivered by an enemy or the trouble discovered when we walk a path God said to avoid. This verse is a declaration that God was faithful, even when King David wasn't.

When you're in trouble—pray. When you recognize trouble—pray. When others are in trouble—*pray*.

God is perfect. His name is perfect. His righteousness is *perfect*. His name should be called out in your spiritual pain. David went as far as reminding God that it wasn't a personal favor to help him out of trouble, but it was for His name's sake. God is the Great Rescuer, and it wouldn't do for God to abandon His title. David couldn't demand to be free from trouble, but he relied on God's own righteousness to find relief from the trouble that dogged his every step.

Jesus said trouble visits all humankind: "In the world you shall have tribulation, but be of good cheer: I have overcome the world" (John 16:33). Face your trouble with or without

God, but you'll still face trouble. You need to decide if facing it alone or with Him is more appealing. If you need help with the right answer, consider Psalm 46:1—"God is our refuge and strength, a very present help in trouble."

Allow your prayer to recognize trouble and then use that same prayer to give your trouble to the one who has a better plan for your worry. As Peter said, cast "all your care upon Him, for He cares for you" (1 Peter 5:7).

Surrender your trouble to God first and always.

Dear God, trouble arrives at the most inconvenient times. I can't plan for it, keep it away, or reschedule it. Trials are common, and as much as I want to avoid them, I want Your help even more. When difficult days come, guide me through each trial. Amen.

POWERFUL PRAYER
Truth # 26

Prayers are uttered by those with enemies.

*And by Your mercy cut off my enemies and destroy
all those who afflict my soul, for I am Your servant.*

PSALM 143:12

Have you ever been broken by the attacks of others, and in a state of weariness you prayed, "Please, make it stop, Lord"?

We've had twelve readings dedicated to a facet of King David's prayer in Psalm 143. What could have made David long so desperately for relief? Some Bible scholars believe this prayer was written when King Saul was trying to kill him.

The good news? God rescued David. He became king, and because he faced so much struggle, he was used by God to provide words of comfort throughout the book of Psalms. Amid the fractured pieces of life, David could say, "The LORD is near to those who have a broken heart and saves those who have a contrite spirit" (Psalm 34:18). You don't serve a God who only meets you once a week in church. God is there for the great mess of actually living.

You have an enemy. It could be physical or spiritual. You've felt the attacks, and you're weary. But as a Christian woman, remember that you have an advocate in the Holy Spirit: "The Spirit also helps our infirmities. For we do not know what we should pray for as we ought, but the Spirit Himself makes intercession for us with groanings that cannot be uttered" (Romans 8:26).

When your enemy seems to be winning and you can't find the words to pray, the Holy Spirit will pray for you—and God's Word will comfort you.

There is real urgency in each word of David's prayer. And because God knew you would face days when DIFFICULTY was the only headline you would see, He made sure this prayer was included. You are not alone.

God, when I'm attacked and left to tend my wounds, stop me from thinking You're too busy to help. You invest in my training, and You rescue Your own. Not every day will be sunshine and roses. You walk with me through storm clouds and trash heaps. Thank You. Amen.

POWERFUL PRAYER
Truth #27

Prayer is a statement of faith.

But without faith it is impossible to please Him, for he
who comes to God must believe that He is, and that
He is a rewarder of those who diligently seek Him.
HEBREWS 11:6

Why would you pray to someone who doesn't exist, can't change things, and has no answers? You probably wouldn't. At a very basic level, prayer is a statement of faith, even if you begin your prayer with, "Lord, I believe; help my unbelief" (Mark 9:24).

Faith is believing before you see the complete truth. You can't please God if you don't believe Him. You can't expect a response to your prayer if you don't believe He exists and that seeking Him is something He rewards.

Sometimes children pray because they see adults pray. They are learning about faith, but they start by modeling what adults do. When they believe God is real and active, they may become more interested in seeking Him.

Faith seems to come easier for children, which may be why Jesus said in Luke 18:16, "Allow little children to come to Me, and do not forbid them, for of such is the kingdom of God." Kids don't need a rational explanation for the tooth fairy. If they are introduced to the idea, they believe it. God is more trustworthy than the tooth fairy—and *He* actually exists.

How can you please God if you deny His existence? How can He reward you if you refuse to look for Him? Yet in God's mercy, He "makes His sun to rise on the evil and on the good, and sends rain on the just and on the unjust" (Matthew 5:45). Maybe God does this so those who don't believe He exists or refuse to look for Him will connect the dots between blessings and believing in the giver.

Pray and declare that the God who has always been and always will be is working to impact the lives of the believer and the yet-to-believe.

Lord God, I pray to You, even though I've never seen You. I ask for Your help, even though I've never heard You with my ears. I do what seems strange to others— because I believe. I've been rewarded through Your blessings, and I've seen Your handiwork in my life. Amen.

POWERFUL PRAYER
Truth #28

Prayer is the answer to what you're seeking.

Seek the LORD and His strength; seek His face continually.
1 CHRONICLES 16:11

Where is the Lord? Where is His strength? Where can you see Him—anytime? These questions should lead to two complementary answers. *Prayer* and *the Bible*.

Let's apply those answers to 1 Chronicles 16:11. *Seek the Lord*—God's Word instructs, reproves, and heals. *Seek the Lord*—your prayers invite His hope, encouragement, and help. *Seek His strength*—His words contain truth, rescue, and authority. *Seek His strength*—your prayers should admit that when you are weak, He is your strength. *Seek His face*—His Word assures you He can be found. *Seek His face continually*—keep praying.

Prayer and the Bible have always been the two sides connecting humankind with God. It's this exact combination that leads to the answers you've always needed. God made a promise for every seeker, that wisdom *can* be found: "I love those who love me, and those who earnestly seek me find me" (Proverbs 8:17).

God can be found. This is key to understanding God. He's not playing a game of hide-and-seek with you. He's not hiding at all. His promise is seek-and-find. Are you willing to seek Him?

If you think God doesn't really mean that, consider Jeremiah 29:13: "And you shall seek Me and find Me, when you search for Me with all your heart."

There's a God worth finding. There's a relationship worth discovering. There's a strength that's available to you. Sometimes, when people say they can't find God it's because they are trying to prove He doesn't exist. They aren't actually looking for Him.

So seek. Find. Follow. Every day of your life.

Father God, I can't find You if I don't seek You.
I won't find answers if I don't look at Your Word.
I don't have access to Your strength if we aren't
friends. We can't be friends if I never accept You.
Help me to find and walk with You. Amen.

POWERFUL PRAYER
Truth #29

Prayer invites protection from temptation.

"Watch and pray, that you do not enter into temptation.
The spirit indeed is willing, but the flesh is weak."
MATTHEW 26:41

Jesus was about to be betrayed. The garden where He prayed would soon be filled with soldiers and the betrayer, Judas. Jesus was about to be killed. But while Jesus thought and prayed over all that would soon take place, His disciples slept.

Three times Jesus asked His disciples to join Him. Each disciple tried. Each failed. Jesus prayed alone, knowing what was about to happen would change everything for humankind.

It's easy to judge the disciples because you know the events that would happen in a very short period of time. It's hard to judge the disciples because *you* have likely fallen asleep while praying.

This was a case of humans being human. They had good intentions but couldn't keep slumber at bay. Jesus would be taken away from them. Do you think they beat themselves up emotionally after the fact? Hadn't Jesus stated clearly that they were in danger of being tempted? He knew they had the willingness; they just didn't have the ability to be anything more than promise breakers.

The biblical account indicates that the disciples fled into the darkness when Jesus was arrested. Yet Jesus didn't abandon them. He worked to restore them so they could be about the business of sharing, following, *and praying*.

Nothing is in God's Word without a reason. You might connect with this verse. Maybe you've felt defeated because you thought it would be easy to follow God, obey, and pray. But it's not, and it hasn't been, and you wonder if it ever will be.

God can rescue you from your best efforts through His faithfulness. He did for three sleepy disciples.

Heavenly Father, You recognize my willingness and weakness. Many times I'll be tempted and fail. You sent Jesus so I could be welcomed and restored every time I break a promise or break trust with You. In those moments, help me pray through my embarrassment. Amen.

POWERFUL PRAYER
Truth #30

Prayer is an expression of joy.

*My heart rejoices in the LORD; my horn is exalted
in the LORD. My mouth is enlarged over my
enemies, because I rejoice in Your salvation.*

1 SAMUEL 2:1

Hannah's husband loved her, but she had been unable to have a child—and she wanted to be a mom.

One year, when Hannah and her husband, Elkanah, visited the temple, she prayed that God would give her a son. But Hannah also did something very unusual: she told God that if He answered her prayer, she would dedicate her son to God's work. The child would be on permanent loan to God.

The priest, Eli, heard her praying and thought she might be drunk. Soon, though, he saw that this was something she had thought deeply about. God would answer her prayer, and a boy named Samuel was born. When he was weaned, Hannah took him to the temple and talked to the same priest she had met a few years earlier. She said, "I am the woman who stood by you here, praying to the LORD. I prayed for this child, and the LORD has given me my petition that I asked of Him. Therefore I have also lent him to the LORD; as long as he lives he shall be lent to the LORD" (1 Samuel 1:26–28).

Then Hannah spoke the words of today's verse, and her

heart erupted in a prayer of pure joy. God had answered her prayer and she fulfilled her vow. There were no shortcuts and no promises broken. Samuel was God's to use, and Hannah was certain her son's future was in the right hands.

When your plans match God's plans, there will always be room for joy. That joy can be shared with others, but it should always be shared with God.

God, it's too easy to look at the world around me and see darkness and pain. Joy seems harder to find and difficult to express. Help me to remember that when Your plans win, I can express joy. Your plans are perfect, and Your joy gives me strength. Amen.

POWERFUL PRAYER
Truth #31

Prayer invites unity.

[Jesus said,] "I do not ask for these alone, but also for those who shall believe in Me through their word, that they all may be one, as You, Father, are in Me, and I in You, that they also may be one in Us, that the world may believe that You have sent Me."

JOHN 17:20–21

Jesus was at the end of His time on earth. Following His crucifixion, the disciples would be scattered, and panic would set in; the men likely felt like fugitives. So Jesus prayed for the unity of the disciples. And His prayer was extended to you too.

Jesus' prayer would be remembered by John the disciple years after Jesus spoke the words. These same words were important enough to be included in the Bible. Perhaps you needed to read them.

Jesus was essentially saying, "I am praying for My disciples, Father. But there will be others who will believe what they say and follow Me too. Make them one because You and I are their example. We are united in thought and purpose. May they join us in a common act of unity. People pay attention to a unified message. May they trust the message that *You* sent *Me*."

There are people who take the message in God's Word and add something, take something away, and in the end, create a belief system that may look a little like Christianity but doesn't encompass all the truth found in God's Word. Paul wrote, "Now I beseech you, brothers, mark those who cause divisions and offenses contrary to the doctrine that you have learned, and avoid them" (Romans 16:17).

You can't be unified with God *and* unified with the ideas of those who don't believe. You can't follow God *and* walk away from Him at the same time. You can't live a life of faith but never trust.

Jesus entrusted good news to faithful people who shared that news with others. They shared the news and eventually you heard it—and believed. Pray for unity and then share what you know.

Father God, there are days when I think it's easier to walk alone. But You ask me to be unified with others who walk with You. You've shown what unity looks like. Help me seek it. Help me find it. Amen.

POWERFUL PRAYER
Truth #32

Prayer is for the bold.

"Oh that You would bless me indeed, and enlarge my territory, and that Your hand might be with me, and that You would keep me from evil, that it may not grieve me!"
1 CHRONICLES 4:10

Have you ever been talking to someone when the discussion took a detour? Your topic is suspended while the other person shares a thought he or she doesn't want to forget. The result seems a little random, and anyone listening may wonder, *What was that all about?*

The book of 1 Chronicles is primarily a book of history. It lists fathers and their sons, tribes and their leaders, a census and some of the people included. Other Bible books might deal with the stories behind the names you read, but this book is not really a source of biblical stories (although there are more than you might think).

First Chronicles 4 introduces us to a man named Jabez. But the verse before any discussion of him reads, "And Koz begot Anub and Zobebah and the families of Aharhel the son of Harum" (verse 8). The verse after reads, "And Chelub the brother of Shuhah begot Mehir, who was the father of Eshton" (verse 11). Why is that important?

God shows up in unexpected places. He remembers His

followers at unlikely times. And when God answers prayer, it's worth an interruption.

All we know about Jabez is found in this chapter. Before his prayer, Jabez is described as honorable. When we read his prayer, we discover he's also bold. And the post-prayer comments tell us that "God granted him what he requested" (verse 10).

Jabez wanted more influence, God's blessing, protection, and favor. So he didn't pray a series of hints. He was bold enough to ask for some of the very things God wants for *you*.

This prayer is not just a bold request; it's a bold desire for a friendship with God. Is it any wonder it needed to be remembered, even in an unlikely place?

Pray that kind of prayer.

Lord, I want to influence other people for You.
Bless me, protect me, and extend Your favor to me.
Help me deal honorably with Your answer to my
prayer. Help me to be a good steward of Your blessings
in my life and use each gift to honor You. Amen.

POWERFUL PRAYER
Truth #33

Prayer is a reminder of God's blessing.

*Blessed is the God and Father of our Lord Jesus
Christ, who has blessed us with all spiritual
blessings in the heavenly places in Christ.*

EPHESIANS 1:3

Maybe you've noticed that God's blessings don't always show up as an unexpected check in the mail, a brand-new car, or the house of your dreams. It can be easy to think that because God made everything, He can give you anything you want—and you'd be happy to call it a blessing.

If that's how it worked, everyone would be rich and selfish. If all you had to do was pray and you'd have more money than you knew what to do with, then everyone would do it. But there are Christians who have very little and are content.

What does Paul mean in this verse?

You have been blessed by God. A simple definition for blessing would be "something God does for you that results in good." You can be blessed when a wayward child returns to a friendship with God. You can be blessed when personal sorrow leads you to seek forgiveness. You can be blessed when God withholds something you want in order to give you something you need.

And what about spiritual blessings? Think about blessings like God's forgiveness, love, salvation, and eternal life. These are among God's greatest ble▓▓▓▓▓▓▓ ▓re priceless! And they should be part of a thanks-for-the ▓▓ssings prayer.

Ephesians 1:3 is the very first part of prayer instruction from the apostle Paul. He suggests praising God for the priceless blessings that every Christian is given yet are often forgotten in favor of something you can own right now.

God is doing something good in your life—call it a blessing.

Lord, Your blessings are new every morning. Your forgiveness, love, salvation, and eternal life have changed me, but sometimes I can forget the things You've done for me that are for my good and Your glory. Let me praise You for these before I ever ask for anything more. Amen.

POWERFUL PRAYER
Truth #34

Prayer is a reminder that God loves you.

*According as He has chosen us in Him before
the foundation of the world, that we should be
holy and without blame before Him in love.*
EPHESIANS 1:4

You love a mountain view. God loves you. You love unexpected meadows. God loves you. You love the shore of a lake. God loves you. While God created all the things you love—*He loves you*. Before the first chirp of a cricket, song of a songbird, or whinny of a horse, God knew your name, had a plan for your life, and loved you more than you could ever love the things He made that you enjoy.

This love, established before the first rotation of the earth, would be enough to make you blameless and set apart for a good purpose in His eyes. His gift to you through Jesus was that Christ became the perfect sacrifice for your sin. Romans 5:8 makes this clear: "But God demonstrates His love toward us, in that while we were still sinners, Christ died for us."

Sometimes people think the Old Testament only shows God's justice and the New Testament suggests He changed His mind and suddenly chose to love humanity. But God's forever love for people should never be in question. Look throughout the Bible and you'll discover God's love for you. Take Zephaniah

3:17: "The LORD your God in the midst of you is mighty. He will save; He will rejoice over you with joy. He will rest in His love; He will rejoice over you with singing." Or this prayer from Psalms: "But You, O Lord, are a God full of compassion, and gracious, long-suffering, and abundant in mercy and truth" (Psalm 86:15).

It's important to remember that the God who made you also loves you. Use prayer to remember that God's love is exceptional.

Father God, I'm grateful for a love that rescued me—for a love that determined to rescue me before I ever had an interest in loving You. May I always remember that Your love allowed us to become friends—and family. May I be quick to show love in return. Amen.

POWERFUL PRAYER
Truth #35

Prayer is a reminder of God's gifts.

*...having predestined us to the adoption of
children by Jesus Christ to Himself, according
to the good pleasure of His will.*

EPHESIANS 1:5

Did you get hung up on the word *predestined*? It's good to know what it means because it helps make sense of God's very personal gift to you.

Have you ever received a piece of mail telling you that you are preapproved for a loan or a credit card? This generally means the bank has determined beforehand that you should have access to its financial products. The problem is you still need to apply, and you could be turned down. In this case, preapproval doesn't guarantee you'll get the loan.

When God says you're predestined, He's saying that because He knew you before you were born, He determined you could be adopted into His family. You could become a child of God. He could make this possible because *He's God*. He offers preapproval.

God doesn't make it hard to accept. Preapproved means you just need to believe, call on Him, and say yes.

The struggle you may have is thinking that, if God determined you could be part of His family, you have no choice in the matter. But Paul wrote "that if you confess with your mouth the Lord Jesus and believe in your heart that God has raised Him from the dead, you shall be saved" (Romans 10:9). God wants to adopt you into His family, and belief signifies your willingness to be adopted.

It's God's pleasure to make you part of His plan. Your prayer can express gratitude that God's plan includes you. You can express thanksgiving that God's salvation was extended to you as one who is preapproved. You can let God know that following Him brings great joy.

---

*Dear God, thank You for predetermining
my ability to become an adopted child in Your
great family. This is a gift I could never expect,
but because it came from You, I would be a fool to
turn it down. Stand by me on the journey. Amen.*

POWERFUL PRAYER
Truth # 36

Prayer is a reminder of God's grace.

*. . .to the praise of the glory of His grace, in which
He has made us accepted in the Beloved.*

EPHESIANS 1:6

The gift described in the last reading is made possible by God's grace. Paul wrote, "For by grace you are saved through faith, and that is not of yourselves; it is the gift of God" (Ephesians 2:8). But just what is grace?

Ephesians suggests that God's grace is glorious, and there's a good reason for that. Grace is a gift that you don't deserve, could never earn, and can't buy. Grace welcomes you into God's family without the need for any kind of pedigree, previous good deeds, or future promise of perfection. God's grace gives without demanding anything except faith. You're rescued by grace when you believe. You can't make this possible on your own. God gave you the gift freely, but it's only a gift if it's accepted.

God's grace was delivered to all humankind, and God's plan for your life is described in Titus 2:11–14: "For the grace of God that brings salvation has appeared to all men, teaching us that, denying ungodliness and worldly lusts, we should live soberly, righteously, and godly in this present world, looking for that blessed hope and the glorious appearing of the great God and our Savior Jesus Christ, who gave Himself for us, that

He might redeem us from all iniquity and purify to Himself a special people, zealous of good works."

Grace gives you what you need most and begins to transform your daily choices to reflect God's character, love, and forgiveness. Seek God's blessed hope, honor the work of Jesus Christ, accept His forgiveness, and submit to His work of purification in your life.

Now that you're reminded of God's grace, spend some time praising God for giving you access to His family simply because He loves you.

Lord, Your grace is amazing. It's a gift that's hard to accept when I don't feel worthy. This gift is freely given because You are worthy. I can't make anything up to You, so help me accept Your forgiveness, embrace Your grace, and take the next step with You. Amen.

POWERFUL PRAYER
Truth #37

Prayer is a reminder of God's redemption.

...in whom we have redemption through
His blood, the forgiveness of sins,
according to the riches of His grace.
EPHESIANS 1:7

Redemption may be a word you've heard but aren't really sure if you understand what it means.

Try this. Imagine you have a collection of paintings. Someone breaks into your home and steals them. They're your paintings, but the thief takes them to a pawn shop and sells them. You pass the pawn shop and see the paintings in the window. You try telling the shop owner that the paintings are yours, but in the end, if you want the paintings back, you'll need to redeem them by paying the full price.

That's what God's redemption is like. He made you, so you *should* be His. But sin removed every human from God. The only way to redeem you was to pay the full price—a life for a life. Jesus became that life. His perfection allowed God to storm Satan's pawn shops and buy back those willing to be redeemed.

Some hesitate and stay on the shelf a little longer, while some always say no. Those who don't want to be redeemed by God will sit, waiting for someone else to redeem them, or they'll try to redeem themselves. But it never happens. God is the only Redeemer, the life-for-life price is just too high, and perfection is required.

God's Son paid the price, and He's willing to redeem us from the dusty shelves.

Use prayer to remember it was God who loved you enough to do the only thing possible to redeem you—a life for a life. Redemption is yours—accept it!

Dear God, with You, I'm redeemed. Without You, I'm sidelined from purpose, praise, and prayer. I'm humbled that You bought me back from my own sin-filled choices. You didn't leave me on the shelf. Help me always remember that Your perfection brings me home. Amen.

POWERFUL PRAYER
Truth #38

Prayer is a reminder of God's wisdom.

...in which He has abounded toward us in all wisdom and prudence.

EPHESIANS 1:8

If God doesn't have answers, then why pray? If He has no way of knowing how to solve your problems, then why ask for help? If the best you can hope for is someone to listen to you, then why ask God for rescue?

Prayer is a great reminder that wisdom has a source, and His name is God. If you are a cup and God's wisdom is water, then He's willing to fill you to overflowing with wisdom, instruction, and understanding. Paul wrote, "All scripture is given by inspiration of God and is profitable for doctrine, for reproof, for correction, for instruction in righteousness" (2 Timothy 3:16).

Ask God for wisdom and expect Him to answer. Your responsibility will be to read the Bible. This is the greatest source of wisdom, instruction, and understanding.

Ephesians 1:8 includes the word *prudence*. God knows you well enough to lavish wisdom in a way that will connect with you. Think of an elementary school math class. Students may be learning how to add single numbers, so the teacher wouldn't try to explain calculus. The students would have large gaps in their knowledge. Similarly, the wisdom God gives is customized for each person. That's prudence: being a good judge of resources and how to use them.

There are some things you'll need to accept as truth before He can teach what you need to know next. There may be things you'll never understand until you meet God face to face in heaven. Why? That will be the place where you'll finally be able to understand the full wisdom of God. Until then, be willing to show God the gratitude He deserves for sharing with you all the wisdom He can today.

Lord, You're wise and Your wisdom is mine for the asking. So, today, I ask. Will You give me wisdom for the choices I make, the relationships I have, and the words I speak? Thank You for making sure I know what I need to know right now. Amen.

POWERFUL PRAYER
Truth #39

Prayer is a reminder of discipleship.

*...having made known to us the mystery
of His will, according to His good pleasure
that He has purposed in Himself.*

EPHESIANS 1:9

God is willing to instruct. Are you willing to learn? God is willing to share wisdom. Are you willing to accept His wisdom as wise? God is willing to teach. Are you willing to attend His class? These are questions that should help you determine if you're willing to be God's disciple (one who learns). Prayer should remind you that you've been given the high honor of gaining insight from God. Sometimes this is called "learning God's will." But what does that mean?

God has a plan and the provision to ensure that His plan succeeds. This is one way to think of God's will. You can know God's plan. It isn't hidden. God *wants* you to do His will, which applies to you, your choices, and your reactions, as well as His people, the world, and everyday events. But God's will is often misunderstood. Maybe that's why Christians need to be long-term learners.

You can cooperate, refuse to help, or stand in the way, but if God wants something done, there's no person or power that can stop Him.

By learning His plan for your own life, you have the opportunity to discover real, personal, meaningful change. Paul advised, "Do not be conformed to this world, but be transformed by the renewing of your mind, that you may prove what is that good and acceptable and perfect will of God" (Romans 12:2).

Learning from God is the start of your transformation. It will require a new way of thinking. You may need to find new friends who are also learning from God. You will need to apply what you learn to your everyday life.

God calls this application process "obedience."

Dear God, You don't want me to be unwise, but You can't teach me when I'm unwilling to learn from You, trust Your plan, and obey Your directions. I want to be Your disciple. I want to follow where You lead and apply what You teach. Amen.

POWERFUL PRAYER
Truth #40

Prayer is a reminder that God has a plan.

...that in the dispensation of the fullness of times He might
gather together in one all things in Christ, both things
that are in heaven and that are on earth, even in Him.

EPHESIANS 1:10

Every country had events that led to the start of that nation. Every marriage had a first date and a mutual "I do." Every man, woman, and child had a moment of birth. But these beginnings are just part of the story. Beginnings are the anchored link to everything that happens next.

In the beginning, God created *everything*. It was the beginning of the collective story of humankind. From the very first human (Adam), humankind insisted on breaking God's law instead of obeying the one who gave them life. But from the moment God breathed life into man, He also had a plan to rescue lawbreakers.

Jesus didn't just come to teach great lessons in good conduct. He didn't come to condemn human beings for the bad choices they make. Jesus came to rescue. But even this was just one thread in a tapestry that depicts the greatest family reunion ever. One day, Jesus will return to take His family home. He wants you to be where He is.

God is gathering His adopted children together into a future

He has planned. In John 14:3, Jesus said, "If I go and prepare a place for you, I will come again and receive you to Myself, that where I am, there you may be also."

Use your prayer time to remember that, above all, Jesus spoke to every Christian when He said, "I give eternal life to them, and they shall never perish, nor shall any man pluck them out of My hand" (John 10:28). This should fill you with a sense of praise. Share your awe with the one whose plan has always been good.

Father God, Your family will gather in eternity because You had a plan. Jesus was always right in the middle of that plan. No one could foil, alter, or interrupt it. I have a life that will exist after death because of it. Thank You for planning. Amen.

POWERFUL PRAYER
Truth #41

Prayer is a reminder of God's salvation.

In Him we also have obtained an inheritance,
being predestined according to the purpose of
Him who works all things according to the counsel
of His own will, that we should be to the praise
of His glory, who first trusted in Christ.
EPHESIANS 1:11–12

Try making the best choices known to man and it won't be enough. Work harder than anyone else and it won't impress. Let's make this easy—there is nothing you can do on your own to make God place your name in His family record. There's only one way to ensure eternal life with God, and that's to accept what Jesus did for you. He's the only reason you have an eternal inheritance.

Ephesians 1:11–12 is very much tied to Jesus and what He's done for you. The verses above follow verse 10 by showing that God has a plan, and that plan has to start with salvation. God's plan isn't just for you but for everyone willing to accept it. It applies to everything because He made all things for His glory.

Let your prayer express gratitude for Jesus' rescue. The same rescue that aligned you with purpose. The same rescue that made you a part of God's family. The same rescue that made you an heiress who will receive an eternal inheritance from God.

You may know about the benefits of forgiveness and God's love, but accepting Jesus opens so many learning opportunities, a secured future, and access to God through prayer.

If this sounds similar to the last reading, you should remember that Ephesians 1:10 assures us that God had a plan that hinged on His Son, Jesus. Verses 11 and 12 make sure you know that God's plan was to rescue you and establish a forever friendship with you.

Father God, what can I do to make things right with You? Jesus already did that. What can I do to impress You? Jesus already did that. Thanks for what Jesus did for me. Work through me because I want to be more like You. Amen.

POWERFUL PRAYER
Truth #42

Prayer is a reminder of God's trustworthiness.

In Him you also trusted, after you heard the word of truth, the gospel of your salvation, in whom also after you believed you were sealed with the Holy Spirit of promise.
EPHESIANS 1:13

You have friends and family members you trust. You trust your car or vacuum or microwave to do their jobs. But people will let you down and things will stop working.

Not so with God. He can be trusted because He's always been trustworthy. Nothing He's promised has been overlooked. Nothing He's said has been proven untrue. His love has never wavered. He has forgiven the faithless, redeemed the worst of wretches, and is preparing a home for the displaced.

It's hard to accept a rescue from someone you don't trust. It's hard to believe the unbelievable. It's hard to have faith in someone who doesn't keep his word. That's why it should be easy to accept, believe, and have faith in God. He's the only one who fits the description. He's the only one who ever has.

Psalm 56:3–4 confirms this. King David wrote, "When I am afraid, I will trust in You. In God (I will praise His word), in God I have put my trust; I will not fear what flesh can do to me."

When you know the one to trust, then His opinion, advice,

and instructions should always have a high priority. The problem is you might find yourself trusting the untrustworthy more than God the faithful. And when people let you down, you can wrongly assume God does the same thing. But He won't. He never has. And He never will.

Prayer is an act of trust. You're praying to someone you've probably never heard speak audibly. You're requesting help from someone you've never seen. You're engaging in a relationship that can seem one-sided. That requires trust—in the trustworthy.

Lord, thank You for the reminders that You can be trusted, that Your Word can be believed, and that Your promises are faithful. When people let me down, help me remember two things. You're always trustworthy and Your Son died for people who break promises. I can trust You forever. Amen.

POWERFUL PRAYER
Truth #43

Prayer is a reminder of heaven.

*...who is the guarantee of our inheritance
until the redemption of the purchased
possession, to the praise of His glory.*

EPHESIANS 1:14

This is the final prayer truth we'll consider from Ephesians 1. We've already learned that prayer is a reminder of God's blessing, love, gifts, grace, redemption, wisdom, discipleship, plan, salvation, and trustworthiness. And once we recognize and accept these things, there's a promised life beyond the one we now live.

Heaven will be the place where you'll *never* be separated from God. Heaven reveals the things we believed while living without actually seeing (see Hebrews 11:1). Heaven is God's home, the place where His family will gather forever. Prayer should remind us that any difficulties we face today cannot be compared to the glory found in the presence of God in heaven (see Romans 8:18).

When older translations of Ephesians 1:14 describe an "earnest" related to your inheritance, it means a pledge or guarantee. If you needed proof that God would redeem you and give you a portion of His righteous inheritance, it would be found in the pledge of His Spirit who works to teach you what you need to know to prepare you for an eternity in heaven. God doesn't remove His Spirit until His family comes home.

Jesus purchased us from the penalty of sin, the Spirit is the promise of heaven, and God receives the praise for coming up with this magnificent plan.

God never needs permission to deliver salvation to the willing. He doesn't take a poll to decide which truths are currently in fashion. He has no reason to consult with humankind on how He makes His plans work. He gave us His Spirit so we will know for certain that His plan wins, heaven is real, and He loves us.

Father God, one day everything I know will change. Heaven will become home, and I'll always be in Your presence. Thank You for Your Spirit who's willing to teach, guide, and walk with me. Your pledge is a guarantee, and Your home will one day be my home. Amen.

POWERFUL PRAYER
Truth #44

Prayer is surrender.

The LORD is near to all those who call on Him, to all who call on Him in truth.

PSALM 145:18

You could pray and not mean it. You could say some words, believing prayer is like rubbing an old lamp in order to get three wishes from a genie. You could humor someone who prays by politely saying something that sounds like a prayer. In each case, God is probably not coming near.

God does come near to those who call on Him in prayer, to those who are intentional about what they are saying—and to whom they are talking. Prayer surrenders personal opinion for a connection with God. It embraces faith and surrenders doubt. It gives up self-reliance for God-reliance.

You might come to this place when you've tried your absolute hardest to manage life on your own, but events have led you to give up your best ideas for God's perfect help. You may have tried self-help or even different beliefs and now conclude that God has the only real answers for life. It's possible that when you were young, you simply chose to believe, and prayer was easy.

God comes near to those who recognize that He exists and decide to come near to Him in prayer. He waits patiently for you to surrender all the choices that have kept you from Him. He wants you to seek Him because, when you do, you *will* find Him.

Surrender is important because, if prayer is just a matter of saying the right words in the right order, then it is little more than a child's memorized bedtime sayings. It lacks relationship because the prayer becomes a ritual and the one praying sees it as just one more thing on her spiritual to-do list.

Dear God, I want my prayer to state that the best answers I'll ever hear come from You. I want my thoughts to be surrendered to Your ideas, commands, and plans. Help me start and end my prayers believing You know more than I ever will. Amen.

POWERFUL PRAYER
Truth #45

Prayer relieves anxiety.

Be anxious for nothing, but in everything,
by prayer and supplication with thanksgiving,
let your requests be made known to God.

PHILIPPIANS 4:6

Prayer is a conversation between you and God. This is the same God who created the world, loved you enough to rescue you, and has a plan for your life.

While this isn't new information, it *is* important because as humbling as it is to come to God with your troubles, you can end the conversation leaving anxiety behind.

There's no shortage of things you could worry about, but Jesus says, "Therefore do not worry, saying, 'What shall we eat?' or 'What shall we drink?' or 'With what shall we be clothed?' For the Gentiles seek after all these things. For your heavenly Father knows that you have need of all these things" (Matthew 6:31–32).

God knows what you need, and He listens when you ask. His eternal emphasis on relationship means you can leave your prayer time feeling worry-free. Maybe the nearest thing to this is when you talk to someone you trust in your family. It could be a parent, grandparent, or sibling. The conversation with this trusted family member calms you and helps set things right in your world—even when that person has no idea how to help solve your problems. God *can* solve your problems, and He's entirely trustworthy. God loves you and specializes in mercy. God has designed a future for you, and He wants you to live it.

Where trust thrives, anxiety has no reason to stay. Make prayer your greatest stress relief. May your requests inspire gratitude. May you let God know everything that concerns you.

You never need to worry when God's in control.

Lord, I can leave my time with You filled with worry, but I don't need to. You take care of me and prove You're capable of managing the details that overwhelm me. Let me be honest, thankful, and willing to let You own my worries. Amen.

POWERFUL PRAYER
Truth # 46

Prayers receive answers.

*[God said,] "And it shall come to pass,
that before they call, I will answer, and while
they are still speaking, I will hear."*

ISAIAH 65:24

Letters sent to Santa might end up in the dead letter department at the post office. Calls to customer service of various companies may be answered by a computer. But prayers are personal and get God's attention.

The psalmist declared, "God has heard me; He has attended to the voice of my prayer. Blessed is God, who has not turned away my prayer or His mercy from me" (Psalm 66:19–20). You need mercy, but you must admit you've done something that requires mercy to receive it.

When you don't admit you missed God's mark of perfection, you can close off communication with God. The psalmist said, "If I regard iniquity in my heart, the Lord will not hear me" (Psalm 66:18). If you have broken God's law but refuse to admit you were wrong, then God can wait until you get honest with Him before answering. He can withhold mercy when you need it the most but are too proud to share your heart with Him.

Many times, God will extend mercy anyway, but that's because He is a patient God. Peter wrote, "The Lord is not slow concerning His promise, as some men count slowness, but is long-suffering toward us, not willing that any should perish but that all should come to repentance" (2 Peter 3:9). Don't trick yourself into thinking it's unimportant to be totally honest with Him.

Today's verse in Isaiah 65 is looking forward to a day of mercy, a moment of turning, a time when the people who sinned would admit they were wrong. When they did, God said He was looking forward to hearing and answering the prayers of those He loved.

Add complete honesty to your prayers. When you blow it—admit it. When you need help—ask. When you want to hide—come out into the open.

God, I wonder if You ever get tired of my failures.
Sometimes I don't want to admit my sin because I
think it will disappoint You, but You already know.
In Your mercy, answer my cry for help. Amen.

POWERFUL PRAYER
Truth # 47

Prayer is a progress report.

*[Jesus prayed,] "I have glorified You on the earth.
I have finished the work that You gave Me to do."*
JOHN 17:4

This book started with the model prayer Jesus taught His disciples. Today you read another prayer from the heart of Jesus.

The Son of God gave His Father a progress report. It was a short report because His human life was soon ending. Jesus mentioned two important things. He had glorified God while living on earth, and He had finished His greatest assignment. This wouldn't have been news to God. He had been following His Son's progress and knew His rescue plan for humankind was about to reach its climax.

Why did Jesus verbalize this in a prayer? See if this helps: If parents want their children to pray before going to bed, they model that behavior by praying first. This may be why Jesus prayed something God already knew. He wanted anyone who followed Him to know He'd been faithful in fulfilling the assignment God had given.

We need this example because sometimes we've been faithful in doing the things God asks us to do, but other times we've blown it and have left things undone. A progress report keeps us honest and authentic. It reminds us of a better direction where our actions are in line with a commendation from God, "Well done, good and faithful servant" (Matthew 25:23).

Using prayer as a progress report can remind you of God's commands, help you clarify what you've been doing, and give direction for the rest of your day.

Glorify God. Be faithful. And finish well.

Father God, I've never really thought about my prayers as progress reports, but since You want to know how things are going in my life, then let me share more than the highlight reel. The big and small things. Thanks for wanting to know about me. Amen.

POWERFUL PRAYER
Truth #48

Prayer invites God's inspection.

O LORD, You have searched me and known me.
PSALM 139:1

You take your car in for service because an annoying light illuminates your dash. Something's wrong. So the technicians connect equipment to diagnose the issue and tell you what needs to be repaired. Usually, you don't second-guess the inspection; you just wonder how you'll pay for the damage.

If humans had dashboard lights, those lights would occasionally indicate that something was wrong. God is the perfect diagnostician. He can search you and knows everything about you. He doesn't need a machine to tell Him what's wrong. He doesn't even need your permission to complete a diagnosis.

Although that could sound frightening, it's actually good news. Before you ever ask for help, God knows what you need. Before you ever acknowledge personal pain, God has the perfect prescription. And before you ever introduce yourself, God knows *everything* about you because you are His beloved daughter.

God can evaluate any human being and knows we'll never measure up. But He also knows He loves us and won't just repair our lives but remake them into something entirely different. Paul wrote, "Therefore if any man is in Christ, he is a new creature. Old things have passed away; behold, all things have become new" (2 Corinthians 5:17).

God is the master designer, and His life plan for you has always been a transformation that restores life, hope, and joy. As you become a new creation, the things you say will change, the way you view others will be altered, and your "check heart light" won't seem to light up as often.

Let God search; He already knows you. And there's no cost for the diagnosis or repairs. Jesus paid for that.

Lord, letting You search and know me feels like a violation of personal space until I understand that You've known me every day of my life and even before that. You don't search me to punish me but to show Your love. Amen.

POWERFUL PRAYER
Truth #49

Prayer acknowledges that God knows everything.

You know when I sit down and when I rise up;
You understand my thought from afar.

PSALM 139:2

Not only does God know and search you, but He reads your mind. He knows what you will do before you do it. There's nothing you can say or do that catches God off guard. *Nothing.*

The upside of this is that God is always with you and knows you better than you know yourself. In John 10:14–15 Jesus said, "I am the good shepherd, and know My sheep, and am known by My own. As the Father knows Me, even so I know the Father, and I lay down My life for the sheep."

Family recognizes family. You're known by God, and God wants you to know Him. You're loved by God, and God wants you to love Him. You receive mercy from God, and God wants you to show mercy.

When you need to take a break, God knows it. When it's time to get back to work, God moves with you into your workplace. When your mind wanders, God can meet you there and help take control of wayward thoughts and give them purpose.

You can't hide from God, and you wore His "masterpiece" stamp before you were even born. Paul wrote, "For we are

His workmanship, created in Christ Jesus for good works, which God has before ordained that we should walk in them" (Ephesians 2:10).

Use your prayer time today to remind yourself that God knows you. He also knows the best plan for today, the steps you'll take tomorrow, and the ones that will one day lead you to your permanent home—and He'll be there to greet you.

Lord, I'm humbled by how familiar You are with me. When I feel guilty because You know the darkest places in my heart, help me remember that Jesus paid the price to bring light to my inner darkness. Shine brightly inside so I can shine brightly outside. Amen.

POWERFUL PRAYER
Truth #50

Prayer recognizes that God is in control.

*You surround my path and my lying down
and get acquainted with all my ways.*

PSALM 139:3

This is day three of a closer look at Psalm 139. You've learned that prayer invites God's inspection and acknowledges that God knows everything. Today you'll be reminded that God is sovereign—He's in control of the past, present, and future. God has never given up control. Not for a second.

God not only knows where you go and when you sleep but also encircles you in His love, protection, and care. The psalmist said, "He shall cover you with His feathers, and under His wings you shall trust. His truth shall be your shield and buckler. You shall not be afraid of the terror by night, or of the arrow that flies by day, or of the pestilence that walks in darkness, or of the destruction that wastes at noonday" (Psalm 91:4–6).

Did you notice the protection offered by God? The Bible has some great word pictures, and these verses are no exception. If you were a baby bird, God would protect you with His wings. If you were a warrior, His truth would protect you like a shield. There is no reason to fear because God can manage nightmares, enemies, sickness, and things that would destroy you.

Troubles and danger are part of the human experience.

Many have died facing enemies, sickness, and personal destruction. But we have hope for something better: "For our light affliction, which is but for a moment, is working for us a far more surpassing and eternal weight of glory" (2 Corinthians 4:17).

Pray to a God who's in control. He's with you in your best and worst moments. He's with you in those "in the middle" times too. And when you face the worst-case scenario, God stays with you no matter the outcome.

Dear God, if there is nowhere I can go to get away from You, then that means You're always with me. If You're always with me, then that means I never face anything alone. If I never face anything alone, then that must mean You love me. Thanks. Amen.

POWERFUL PRAYER
Truth #51

Prayer admits that words are important.

For there is not a word on my tongue,
but behold, O LORD, You know it altogether.

PSALM 139:4

This book contains thousands of words. Each word was linked with another in an effort to create thoughts that make sense and honor God. Before the words were ever typed, they had to form in the heart and mind—and God knew exactly what those words would be.

Words are so important to God that He keeps track of what you say. He watches as you say mean things to or about others. He's beside you listening if you choose to use His name as a profanity.

James wrote, "But no man can tame the tongue; it is an unruly evil, full of deadly poison. With it we bless God, even the Father, and with it we curse men who are made in the likeness of God" (James 3:8–9). From the same mouth you use to praise God, words can form that hurt others. God is aware that you'll use your words this way, and He hears the words that damage men, women, and children made in His image.

Yet this isn't a book of condemnation. God's grace continues to pull you toward Him. As you learn from God, you will alter the choice of your words. No Christian is where she wants to be, needs to be, or will one day be. Change will take place when you move where God is leading you. Your words can speak life—that's a truth God knows about you too.

Father God, You hear when I gossip, say cruel things, or speak untrue words. I'm sorry my words have hurt others. I'm sorry my words have hurt You. Help me pay attention to Your Word so what I say can be transformed by Your grace. Amen.

POWERFUL PRAYER
Truth # 52

Prayer knows God orchestrates life.

*You have surrounded me behind and before and
laid Your hand on me. Such knowledge is too
wonderful for me; it is high; I cannot attain it.*

PSALM 139:5–6

Smartphone apps allow parents to track their children. Parents
can know where their kids are at any time as long as they
have their phones with them. Some parents may feel this is
an invasion of privacy and would never use such a tool. Other
parents may think it's a wise use of technology that might help
keep their children safe.

God leads and guides you, and He knows whether you'll
actually follow. He knows where you are at any moment because
He never leaves your side. Prayer can gratefully acknowledge
that God watches over you and watches out for you.

Follow in faith, run in rebellion, or rest in a rocking chair,
but God has a specific set of directions, and you must choose
whether you'll follow those directions, whether you'll "lay aside
every weight, and the sin that so easily besets us, and let us
run with patience the race that is set before us" (Hebrews 12:1).

If life is an orchestra, then God is the conductor. He knows
how to unify His family, bring them to a point of harmony,
and inspire those who have been unsure about joining His

orchestra. God just knows how to make things work in a way that surprises, amazes, and pleases those who thought nothing good could come from a bad circumstance, choice, or thought.

You now know that nothing surprises God because He knows everything—from what you will say to where you will go, from what you do to what you'll become. This can and should invite a sense of wonder because it means God isn't going anywhere. He never abandons you.

Lord, You protect me from all angles. No matter where I come from or where I go, You take steps with me, even when I'm off track. When I follow You, I'm led to a better place, future, and hope. You are majestic. Amen.

POWERFUL PRAYER
Truth #53

Prayer welcomes the closeness of God.

Where shall I go from Your Spirit? Or where shall I flee from Your presence? If I ascend up into heaven, You are there. If I make my bed in hell, behold, You are there. If I take the wings of the morning and dwell in the uttermost parts of the sea, even there Your hand shall lead me and Your right hand shall hold me.

PSALM 139:7–10

Get away from it all. Find the most remote place on earth. Hide in the deepest cave you can find. Keep running away from everything you know. Try it if you must.

But if your goal is to distance yourself from God, your plan is doomed from the start.

God knows you, loves you, and never leaves you, so when you try to take a break from God's influence in your life, you're asking Him to do what He can't—what He won't. He didn't create you to abandon you. He doesn't give up parental rights to watch you run toward chaos and destruction. He won't just throw up his hands in exasperation and say, "Well, I tried."

If you find yourself on a remote island, you can expect God to show you the beauty He created for you to enjoy. Take in a view from a mountaintop and become overwhelmed by the grand vista that He created with His words. Watch the world from the height of a skyscraper and be confronted with the truth that God created the people who form the bustle below your observation deck.

The apostle Paul reemphasized this love when he wrote in Romans 8:38–39, "For I am persuaded that neither death nor life, nor angels nor principalities nor powers, nor things present nor things to come, nor height nor depth, nor any other creature shall be able to separate us from the love of God that is in Christ Jesus our Lord."

Use your prayer time today to welcome the closeness of God—the one who won't let places, events, people, or even your past keep you from His love.

God, You're mighty, You're victorious, and You are for me. I'm grateful that no matter where I go today, You go with me. I'm honored that I mean so much to You that we're traveling companions. You lead, and I'll follow. Amen.

POWERFUL PRAYER
Truth #54

Prayer believes God controls dark days.

*If I say, "Surely the darkness shall cover me, even the
night shall be light around me," yes, the darkness does
not hide from You, but the night shines as the day.
The darkness and the light are both alike to You.*

PSALM 139:11–12

When the sun fades, some people are uncomfortable being
outside. Most crimes are committed at night. There are even
some locations where people are advised to stay indoors when
darkness arrives. If that sounds ominous, just think about
what Jesus said: "And this is the condemnation, that light has
come into the world, and men loved darkness rather than light,
because their deeds were evil" (John 3:19).

Darkness hides moments when you give in to your worst
impulses. Or does it? Darkness hides moments when people
are cruel to each other. Or does it? Darkness makes it harder
for anyone to know what you're doing. Or does it?

Psalm 139 makes it clear—darkness hides nothing from God.
The psalm confirms that God walks with you no matter what.
He knows your thoughts. He knows what you'll say. He knows
where you go. And God doesn't need night vision goggles. He
brings light to all circumstances, and darkness never leaves
Him feeling uncomfortable.

If Satan is defined by darkness and God is defined by light, then it's good to remember that darkness *can't* eliminate a light source, but light *always* removes darkness. Rejoice in prayer, knowing God's light always surpasses any darkness Satan brings with him. Your darkest days are no match for God's light. Because He never leaves or forsakes you, His light always cuts through whatever darkness encroaches on your day.

John 8:12 is a bold declaration from Jesus: "I am the light of the world. He who follows Me shall not walk in darkness but shall have the light of life." When real or figurative darkness arrives, just remember that God works the night shift, that He takes care of you while you sleep, and that the God who reminds you to "fear not" is the same God who knows no fear.

Father God, fear seems to be born in the darkness. I can become afraid of the things I've never encountered and can't see a way through. You don't have this problem. Darkness means nothing to You. Thanks for bringing light to my unknown. Amen.

POWERFUL PRAYER
Truth # 55

Prayer remembers that God made you.

*For You have formed my inmost being. You have
woven me in my mother's womb. I will praise You,
for I am fearfully and wonderfully made. Marvelous
are Your works, and my soul knows that very well.*

PSALM 139:13–14

Artists can take tubes of color and create a treasured painting.
Home builders can take wood, nails, and a hammer and create
a beautiful dream home. A talented mechanic can take a car
you once owned and make it even better than new. While these
artisans can make for memorable reality TV shows, they can't
hold a candle to the God who made you.

A painting might be able to speak to you in an artistic sense,
but it can't carry on a conversation. If heaven is your real home,
then a dream house on earth is only temporary living quarters.
A custom car can evoke great memories, but it is little more
than mobile art.

God made you with a mind, heart, and soul. He invites you
to take all three and add your strength to the way you love
Him (Mark 12:30). He made you in His image (Genesis 1:26).
He delights in hearing you pray (Proverbs 15:8).

The body God created for you has a shelf life. It will end.
But while you live, your body is perfectly equipped to pray. You

can think; you can understand. God loves to hear from you, and His wisdom is yours for the asking.

Think of the things you can make with your hands. Can you create a living being that you can talk with, teach, and reason with? If you're thinking of a child, you may technically be correct, but God is the only one who has ever made a human—even those who refuse to acknowledge Him. John 1:3 makes this clear: "All things were made by Him, and without Him nothing was made that was made."

Dear God, You're an artist, life builder, and custom designer. I'm not exactly like anyone else and You call me a masterpiece. You made me to be creative. The only improvement I can make on myself happens as I let You work in me. Amen.

POWERFUL PRAYER
Truth #56

Prayer acknowledges that life is God's gift.

*My substance was not hidden from You when I was
made in secret and skillfully formed in the lowest
parts of the earth. Your eyes saw my substance,
yet being imperfect, and in Your book all my
members were written, which in continuance were
fashioned, when as yet there were none of them.*

PSALM 139:15–16

Each of us has a date of birth. We celebrate it every year. But this is *not* the date of life. That was planned by God before it was known by our parents. He had a baby book prepared before our first sonogram.

This isn't a political statement—it's the heart of Psalm 139:15–16. When you were growing inside your mother's womb, God wasn't surprised by your existence. *He was already planning for your future.* When no one was looking and when nobody knew, God saw you, knew your name, and formed you. God did something similar with the first person, Adam: "And the LORD God formed man from the dust of the ground and breathed into his nostrils the breath of life, and man became a living soul" (Genesis 2:7).

When you had no skill, couldn't talk, and were still being formed, the greatest artist this world will ever know added all the beautiful touches that make you who you are. Matthew 6:26 adds some perspective: "Behold the fowls of the air, for they do not sow; they neither reap nor gather into barns. Yet your heavenly Father feeds them. Aren't you much more valuable than they are?"

The life you've been given is a gift, and the prayers you pray can express gratitude to God for a new day that will be filled with opportunities to advance the purpose for which you were made.

No child is hidden from God, and every child is important to Him. You were once a child. You are still important to God. You are not hidden from Him. He sees you, knows you, and loves you.

Father God, it's easy to think You care about some people but maybe not me. Thanks for the reminder that there's no one who's unimportant to You. There's no one You didn't design with a good plan and purpose. You've already proven Your love and I'm overwhelmed. Amen.

POWERFUL PRAYER
Truth #57

Prayer acknowledges that God thinks of you.

How precious also are Your thoughts to me,
O God! How great is the sum of them! If I were to
count them, they would be more in number than
the sand. When I awake, I am still with You.

PSALM 139:17–18

Parents and grandparents often gush about their children and grandchildren. Every achievement, no matter how small, is recalled with all the skill and enthusiasm of the great storytellers. Sometimes the story connects with those who hear it; other times it mostly means more to the teller.

This is a picture you can apply to how God thinks of you. He has stories about you that He could share with anyone who is willing to listen. He knows about kindnesses you showed that seemed to go unnoticed, love that bore a family resemblance, and sacrifice that proved you've been paying attention to His plan for you.

It's true, you won't always follow directions, you'll need to be rescued, and you'll miss the mark of God's perfection. But none of that diminishes the wonderful memories God has of you.

God created you for relationship. He created everything else for you to enjoy. Nehemiah 9:6 is a prayer to the God who thinks about you: "You, even You, are LORD alone. You have made heaven, the heaven of heavens, with all their host, the earth and all things that are in it, the seas and all that is in it, and You preserve them all. And the host of heaven worships You."

Tomorrow when you wake up, or perhaps even at this moment, remember that God is with you—and you're on His mind. He loves you and He thinks of you often. He has a good plan for you, and He knows how far you can go. He has memories of you, and He calls them precious.

Lord, when I think of You, I'm led to a place of praise. You're more wonderful than anything I've ever encountered. I'm amazed that You ever give me a thought. Yet You do. You think of me more often than I think of You. I'm humbled. Amen.

POWERFUL PRAYER
Truth #58

Prayer invites God into every part of life.

*Search me, O God, and know my heart; test me,
and know my thoughts, and see if there is any wicked
way in me, and lead me in the way everlasting.*

PSALM 139:23–24

The verses you just read are the finale of the Psalm 139 prayer. At first blush, it may seem that it's a simple acknowledgment that God knows everything; but if that's the only thing you take away from these verses, then you've missed some very rich truth layers.

Search me: An invitation. A voluntary request for a divine assessment. A statement of intimacy that proclaims that God is welcome to see who you really are. God can do this anytime He wants, but the psalmist sent out an invitation. This is trust.

Know my heart: You were born with a deceitful heart. Only God can know how bad it really is. This isn't a dare prayer, as if challenging God to find your imperfection. This is an acknowledgment of imperfection and a request for personal change.

Test me, and know my thoughts: Your mind can take you to places you wish you hadn't visited. Ask God for a report on your spiritual health. God has a remedy for your choices, and He's willing to help.

See if there is any wicked way in me: This is a bold request because God *will* uncover the wickedness in you.

Lead me in the way everlasting: This is a perfect ending to this insightful prayer. God sees, knows, and never leaves. It is a picture of a child reaching a hand toward a parent when she is totally unsure of what lies ahead. What that child knows, what the psalmist learned, and what can change the course of your walk with God is that He can be trusted with what He knows about you.

God wants to be included in every part of your life. Let Him. His involvement always brings healing. Your prayer can be His invitation.

God, Your way is better than mine. Having You lead is always my best choice. When I allow You to diagnose my spiritual health, I know You'll find problems I brought on myself. But instead of condemning me, You work to restore what's been damaged. Amen.

POWERFUL PRAYER
Truth #59

Prayer is a command.

Continue in prayer.

COLOSSIANS 4:2

What kind of power would prayer have if it was downgraded to *optional*? Imagine if the words found in scripture urged you to pray only when it made you feel better, when it wasn't awkward, or when you'd run out of options, so praying was a last-ditch effort.

God made prayer a command without any qualifications—not some of the time, not just when in trouble, not as a ritual before meals. God commanded you to pray continually.

If that sounds heavy-handed, you probably have the wrong view of this command. God made sure you could know what He thought by giving you His Word. Relationships are important to Him, so He made sure you had a way to talk to Him, and then added some motivation to do so.

On your own, you probably would find no need to pray. You might think it's unnatural to talk to someone you can't see. You might even think it's unnecessary to pray since God has supplied answers in the Bible.

But can you have a relationship with someone you refuse to talk to? Does a marriage or a friendship grow if the people in it won't communicate? When you're told to continue in prayer, the end goal is closeness through obedience. Read any of the prayers in the Psalms and you'll begin to see that closeness and love expressed through prayer.

There's a full menu of benefits associated with prayer. If you treat prayer like something you check off to make God happy, then you miss so many good things that can happen when a daughter of God spends time with her Father.

Lord, I want to be close to You. I don't want to feel as if I'm trying to fill a quota when I pray to You. I want this to be my part of a conversation—connecting my heart to Yours in a way that's better than I expected. Amen.

POWERFUL PRAYER
Truth #60

Prayer connects you with others.

*For God, whom I serve with my spirit in the gospel
of His Son, is my witness that without ceasing I
always make mention of you in my prayers.*

ROMANS 1:9

In the last reading, you learned that God has a reason for commanding His people to pray. Today's reading connects perfectly with this command. You should pray because by doing so, other people become important to you.

The apostle Paul wrote, "Let nothing be done through strife or boastfulness, but in lowliness of mind let each esteem others better than themselves" (Philippians 2:3). Since other people should be esteemed highly, their concerns should play a key role in your prayer life. That kind of prayer indicates that God's love has changed you enough that reaching out to others is more natural than most believe possible. If your prayer life is all about you, take comfort in knowing that God will be working on you to join the fellowship of the faithful.

Christians who pray with and for others know that when God is concerned about one prayer, He is concerned about all prayers. Why? He's concerned about all people.

Paul, in Colossians 1:9, said, "For this reason we also, since the day we heard it, do not cease to pray for you and desire that you might be filled with the knowledge of His will in all wisdom and spiritual understanding." Who wouldn't want to know someone is praying that kind of prayer for them? You can do that for others. They can do it for you. It was God's idea.

Praying for others typically brings people together. It's a way to stand with someone. It leaves no one out; no one behind. Maybe you've never thought of prayer as an act of love, but the evidence is clear. Love does that. Love prays.

Dear God, I can be so concerned about the issues I face that I forget there are other people around me who have needs, carry burdens, and have no idea how to manage their personal crises. Help me love them enough to pray for them. Amen.

POWERFUL PRAYER
Truth #61

Prayer and obedience go together.

And whatever we ask we receive from Him,
because we keep His commandments and do
those things that are pleasing in His sight.

1 JOHN 3:22

There are some things to consider when reading the verse above. The first half can make it sound like prayer is placing a card in a suggestion box, believing your suggestion will be taken as the highest priority. *Not true.* Conditions and exclusions apply.

God can—and does—answer prayer. His Word can—and does—say that when you ask for something, you can expect to receive it. But God adds some clarification. He answers prayers when those who pray keep His commands and follow His lead.

If you choose sin over God's will, He can't reward disobedience. It's a bad policy for parents and something God has never wavered on.

Obedience to God's commands is always linked to the way God answers prayer. Paul asked, "Do you not know that the one to whom you yield yourselves as servants to obey, you are his servants to whom you obey, whether of sin to death, or of obedience to righteousness?" (Romans 6:16).

Sin separates you from God. Obedience re-establishes a broken connection.

God's positive answers to your prayers are connected to a transformation of the heart—one that leaves selfishness behind in favor of requests God wants to answer. When you were a child, you probably wouldn't have asked your parents for something you knew they objected to. Why ask God for something you know He will reject? You can't ask God for something He has commanded you not to do and expect Him to say yes. You can't ask God to deny who He is in order to do something you know is wrong. Ask and receive but know God well enough to ask for something He wants to give. Obedience is your starting point.

Lord, when I call You by that name, I'm saying You're in charge. Your rules are right, Your ways are righteous, and Your answers are perfect. Help me obey You so I will begin to pray in keeping with Your will. Amen.

POWERFUL PRAYER
Truth #62

Prayer wants what God wants.

Delight yourself also in the LORD, and He
shall give you the desires of your heart.

PSALM 37:4

When God becomes your everything, you can expect your desires to change. Prayer does not want what God does not want. Beyond obedience, this prayer truth insists that the closer you get to God, the closer your prayers will reflect His heart.

This dynamic is a prime directive and an attainable goal; it matches God's plan when it comes to your friendship with Him. Imagine how pleased God is when His children begin praying prayers He's most interested in saying yes to. This doesn't mean having no choice in the subject matter of your prayers because God wants to hear everything you have to say. It does mean that God is so important to you that your prayers for yourself and for others all seem bathed in understanding God's involvement in your lives.

If you're new in your faith, you can expect some missteps in how you ask. If you've been a Christian for a while, you can still expect missteps. But when you're sold out to God's plan for you—as well as society at large—it becomes much easier to avoid certain prayers that not only are unproductive but also result in God saying no.

This step beyond obedience is a special relationship between best friends. While other people make educated guesses, you can be more certain about God and His actions and His reactions to the choices you make. Just as Paul advised, "Therefore do not be unwise, but understand what the will of the Lord is" (Ephesians 5:17).

Find your greatest delight in the God who made you. He wants you to know Him and to share life with Him. He wants to work with you to unfold the passionate pursuit of purpose He offers with every answered prayer.

Father, change my desires to match Your plan.
Hold my heart as I follow Your lead. Call me friend
as I call You Lord. Help me want what You want
because what You want is exactly what I need.
Even when I'm uncertain, help me trust You. Amen.

POWERFUL PRAYER
Truth #63

Prayer holds God in high esteem.

*I cried to Him with my mouth, and He
was extolled with my tongue.*

PSALM 66:17

What happens when you find yourself in desperate situations? Some people resort to desperate acts that may have long-term negative consequences. Others turn to God because their desperation is no match for His wise intervention.

You can use your mouth to admit that you can't do life on your own. Words can request help, acknowledge failure, and seek wisdom. Like the psalmist's words, your words might come like a cry to the ears of a loving God who always knows how to comfort.

You may cringe at the comparison, but crying out is how babies get the care they need. If their diaper requires a change, they cry. The same is true for pain, fear, or hunger. When they don't know how to ask for what they need, they resort to a throaty cry that is a universal distress call.

Those same babies can smile, hug, and kiss their parents when their needs are met. This is the childlike equivalent of the Christian who extols God with her tongue. To extol means to rave about or praise enthusiastically. God meets needs and deserves your high esteem.

Prayer is an understanding that even before you cry out to God for help, you're certain that He's amazing. Talking *about* Him while talking *to* Him never seems a great enough response, yet it's fully appropriate. That's why praise should be mobile. It should be easy to move praise from your prayer life to the songs you sing. Paul urged believers to join with others in "speaking. . .in psalms and hymns and spiritual songs, singing and making melody in your heart to the Lord" (Ephesians 5:19).

When desperate, esteem God highly; praise Him deeply.

*Dear God, I think of Your goodness, and I'm
undone. I think of my need, and in desperation,
I cry out to You. I'm not able to manage every
detail of life alone. Help me and accept my esteem.
Walk with me and hear my praise. Amen.*

POWERFUL PRAYER
Truth #64

Prayer is hindered by sin.

If I regard iniquity in my heart, the Lord will not hear me.
PSALM 66:18

Do you ever pray and get the feeling that God isn't listening?
He could just be saying no for now, but sometimes our calls
to God seem blocked. There's a reason why this happens. *Sin.*

A common belief is that if you're a sinner, God will not
hear your prayer. But if that's true, then who could be saved?
Everyone sins.

This verse may be best understood as something applied
to Christians. The psalmist could have said, "When I let sin
have a guest room in my heart, the Lord will not enable me
to continue to sin. His silence says it all." There's a barrier
separating your prayer from God's answer when you sin and
refuse to deal with it. Your prayers seem to fall on deaf ears.

You can't work your way out of a sinful condition, but you
can admit that God is right, and you've been wrong. You can
confess your sin and accept God's forgiveness.

The problem many Christians experience is thinking they
get to define sin. They want an exception clause or loophole.
They don't mind God's law as applied to other people; they just
don't want it applied to their choices.

But God sets the standard. You either live up to the standard or admit you didn't. You're either perfect or admit you aren't. You either refrain from sin or admit you haven't.

Sin is a prayer repellent if, instead of confessing it, you sweep it under the rug. You might promise yourself you'll do better next time; you might try to pay God back with acts of charity or balance the scale of justice using your own standards. These things have never worked. If you sin, you have one acceptable choice—admit it in prayer.

Lord, even the sin I think is small is a big deal to You. Things I think are minor infractions can prevent my prayers from reaching You—not because You don't care about me, but because I'm too proud to admit You're right and I'm wrong. Amen.

POWERFUL PRAYER
Truth #65

Prayer can move God to action.

*But truly God has heard me; He has
attended to the voice of my prayer.*

<small>PSALM 66:19</small>

After the psalmist's admission that sin puts up walls to answered prayer, he wrote that God has heard his prayers—and He's done something about them.

This a joy prayer. Why? The communication connection has been reestablished! There has to be joy in knowing that a closeness continues because we are willing to admit that breaking any law of God is wrong.

Take the time to read through Psalm 19:7–14. Turn it into a prayer. It could sound something like this: "Father, Your law is perfect. Your testimony is sure. Your statutes are right and commandments pure. Your judgments are true—they are completely righteous. I want God-truth that is more valuable than gold and sweeter than honey. Your words send up warning signals, and You reward those who pay attention and take action. I will sin, but I want Your roadblocks to break the habit. Don't let rebellion be the king of my life. I want what I think and say to bear Your stamp of approval. In You, I find strength. In You, I'm redeemed."

God is moved to action when someone prays a prayer that

admits that He is perfect and wise and has the final word. This kind of prayer acknowledges that the God who made everything makes the rules. This is the kind of prayer that knows that the God who makes the rules loves us and has made a way for us to talk with Him.

Peter wrote, "For the eyes of the Lord are on the righteous, and His ears are open to their prayers, but the face of the Lord is against those who do evil" (1 Peter 3:12). God hears you—make sure you hear Him.

Lord, let me fully embrace the truth that Your Word is right and holds the answers to my questions. Help me to remember that You hear me when I pray the prayer of someone who believes You are the final word. Amen.

POWERFUL PRAYER
Truth #66

Prayer means the lines of communication are open.

*Blessed is God, who has not turned away
my prayer or His mercy from me.*

PSALM 66:20

Be stubborn. Resist God's love. Reject His great rescue plan. Tell Him He's phony, outdated, and irrelevant. Do all these things and more and, in the end, God might still offer mercy instead of judgment, hope instead of desperation, and love instead of retribution.

Peter was perhaps Jesus' most impulsive disciple. He spoke before he thought and made promises he couldn't keep; but sometimes, when he got something right, this disciple acted as if he was the teacher's pet. Once, when Peter came to Jesus, he said, "Lord, how often shall my brother sin against me and I forgive him? Up to seven times?" Jesus replied, "I do not say to you, up to seven times, but up to seventy times seven" (Matthew 18:21–22).

This short exchange was put in the Bible for a reason. It wasn't to put Peter in his place, but to instruct you today—at this moment, at this time—that God has experienced what Peter described. If you ever wondered if there was a limit on the times He could forgive you, His actions indicate He stopped counting. His forgiveness and mercy have been dedicated to your need for forgiveness and mercy. God isn't paying attention to the number of times you've stumbled, the sheer volume of requests you've made for mercy, or the prayers that start with, "Hey God, it's me again." God is paying attention *to you*.

God wants to keep the lines of communication open. He knows you'll need to talk, and He wants you to talk. He's aware of any self-loathing and He offers kindness. He doesn't want you to hide like Adam and Eve did. God wants you to come as you are and leave changed by His mercy—*transformed by His love*.

Dear God, I can be impulsive like Peter and need forgiveness. I can think I'm being gracious but still have judgment in my heart. Your forgiveness and love never end and offer a great example for me to follow. Help me always to communicate with You and others. Amen.

POWERFUL PRAYER
Truth #67

Prayer includes community.

I exhort therefore, first of all, that supplications, prayers, intercessions, and giving of thanks be made for all men.
1 TIMOTHY 2:1

The apostle Paul wrote letters to Timothy because Timothy was young and would become a leader in the church. He needed instruction, and that's exactly what Paul offered in these two small books: 1 Timothy and 2 Timothy.

First Timothy 2:1–4 provides some solid prayer advice for a young pastor and everyone that would ever read these verses. When a Bible passage says *therefore*, it's always an answer to information provided in the preceding verses. In this case, Paul urged Timothy to fight the good fight of faith, grip faith with a strong hand and clean conscience, and be aware that there are some who will seek to sabotage God's work.

That's the backdrop and the reason Paul said that "supplications, prayers, intercessions, and giving of thanks be made for all men" (verse 1). This might sound unfair and even a little unwise. You probably know someone you don't think deserves the time it takes you to pray. You'll have reasons that justify why praying for *those* people or *that* person makes no sense. You're probably willing to act on your faulty reasoning and maybe even claim that God doesn't fully understand your particular situation.

Prayers for the good, the bad, and the unjust end up helping everyone. God can take your humble requests, thoughtful prayers, interventions on behalf of others, and every expression of gratitude and use them to strengthen you and invite others to seek Him. This is the essence of community. It's not about keeping sinners at arm's length. It's inviting sinners to see the outstretched arms of Jesus, to recognize that the kindness they see in you is God's kindness that can lead them to repentance (see Romans 2:4).

Do you want to improve your community? Pray for the most unlikely. They need your prayers.

Lord, it's easy to discount the need to pray for sinners who annoy me. It's simple to believe that some people are impossible to be around and that praying for them would just be for show. May I pray for my community—even the most unlikely and seemingly impossible. Amen.

POWERFUL PRAYER
Truth #68

Prayer includes leaders.

. . .for kings and for all who are in authority, that we may lead a quiet and peaceful life in all godliness and honesty.

1 TIMOTHY 2:2

You've probably voted in an election in which your candidate of choice lost. You're not enthusiastic about the person who was elected. You could spend your time hoping for something better in the next election. . .or you could pray for the person who was elected.

It's easy to let political arguments place a wedge between friends. Paul had a different idea and urged Timothy never to let the forward movement of faith be stopped by arguments over governmental affairs. Instead of engaging in a verbal battle over the wisdom of government rules, pray for those who lead. You might notice this verse doesn't say to pray *against* them but *for* them.

This verse also lists a positive result of following its directive. When politics are less important than the God who rules the affairs of humankind, there's a greater possibility of leading a quiet and peaceable life.

God is more interested in believers learning to follow Him than in having us follow political polls, personality profiles, and policy provisions. Good citizens are informed, and they vote. But for the Christian woman, real citizenship is in heaven (Philippians 3:20). If politics surpass the level of Christian passion and pursuit, then it's essentially idolatry because we've given politics a place greater than God in our lives.

Be encouraged. You can be involved in politics and be a Christian. You can be a mayor and follow Christ. Christians can and should express good citizenship. Just remember that your relationships with God, family, and other people are always going to be more important than joining a protest or writing a letter to the editor.

Father God, it can be easy to make opinions about governmental decisions more important than You. The issues of today are no match for the future You have for me. Help me to remember that no matter what happens, You've never given up control. Amen.

POWERFUL PRAYER
Truth #69

Prayer pleases God.

*For this is good and acceptable in
the sight of God our Savior.*
1 TIMOTHY 2:3

In the last two readings, you've learned some prayer directives delivered from God to Paul and Timothy to you: pray for those in your community and pray for leaders. *Why?* "For this is good and acceptable in the sight of God our Savior."

Prayer pleases God. The things you pray for can be an indicator of growth, understanding, and a willingness to take what you know and do something with it.

The apostle Paul wrote, "We beseech you, brothers, and exhort you by the Lord Jesus, that as you have received from us how you ought to walk and to please God, so you would abound more and more" (1 Thessalonians 4:1). Your time in prayer should improve as you continue your conversation with God. Transformation happens through obedience, and prayer is a facet of obedience that can help lead you to make the kind of decisions God would make. These decisions please God.

God has done everything needed to create and maintain a connection with you. It's your responsibility to take what He's given and actually use it to communicate in return. When you care enough to talk to the God who forgives you and offers His love, it signifies that the very things God gave you are being received—and that too pleases God.

The idea of pleasing God is not about brownie points, gold stars, or personalized awards. It's not like a child hoping that good behavior translates to candy, ice cream, or a new toy. Pleasing God is about His influence changing everything about you, including how you treat everyone else.

Dear God, finding those things that are good and acceptable to You will mean I have to understand the way You want things done. As I pray, may my words describe a growing love for those You have created—the people You love, the very people You want me to love. Amen.

POWERFUL PRAYER
Truth #70

Prayer acknowledges God's plan for others.

*. . .who wants all men to be saved and to
come to the knowledge of the truth.*
1 TIMOTHY 2:4

Did God send Jesus to rescue some while leaving others with
no chance of being saved? Did Jesus come to proclaim truth
only to a select few? How can you be sure?

God would love to see salvation come to all people. Paul told
young Timothy that it's God's desire that no one is held back
from knowing His truth. *Not a single person.*

His love is limitless. His rescue plan is universally available.
His faithfulness has never once skipped a generation. He's for
all people—even the ones you don't like.

Your prayer life should acknowledge that if God has a plan
for you, then He has a plan for everyone else. If He wants the
best for you, then He wants the best for everyone else. If God
wants to see you rescued from sin, then He wants the same
thing for everyone else. Pray with the awe of one who recognizes that all people were created by God and have equal
opportunity to become part of His family. In Acts 10:34–35,
the apostle Peter said, "Truly I perceive that God shows no
partiality, but in every nation he who fears Him and works
righteousness is accepted by Him."

Sharing your faith may be the first step in someone else discovering God's plan. When you keep God to yourself, you're holding back blessings for yourself because wanting what God wants means wanting His plan for others to come true.

Don't withhold Jesus from others because they're different. Don't believe that anyone is too far away from God to discover new life. And don't be afraid of what people think. It's always been true that God's opinion should be held in the highest esteem because His opinion matters most.

Father, You know me better than anyone ever could. Nothing is hidden from Your notice. You came for all mankind. When I object, remind me that everyone has been outside looking in. I found You—look out for those who are still on the outside looking in. Amen.

POWERFUL PRAYER
Truth #71

Prayer remembers Jesus.

For there is one God and one mediator between
God and men, the man Christ Jesus.

1 TIMOTHY 2:5

If you were charged with a crime, you'd want an attorney to represent you, right? You'd probably want your attorney to be completely aware of the issues you face. Chances are good that you'd want to talk to your attorney before the judge heard your case.

Prayer grants you access to your spiritual attorney. When you're guilty of breaking God's law—and we're *all* guilty—you need someone to represent you in God's court. There's only one who can fight for you, and you don't even need to call a toll-free number to see if He'll represent you. Just pray. Just ask. Just trust.

Without the help only Jesus can offer, you face the death penalty. He has an argument that will set you free every time. When you accept Jesus, you accept a mediator, advocate, and go-between. God perfectly understands the case Jesus presents and it changes everything.

Jesus came to earth, died on a cross as the only perfect sacrifice for humankind, and defeated death. When you stand condemned, Jesus simply says, "I paid the price for that broken law." *That truth is enough.* You get mercy when justice was expected, forgiveness in place of a lawful conviction, and hope when living on death row.

You're *not* found acceptable to God based on your best efforts. You're accepted as perfect before God because Jesus offered His perfection for your "not guilty" verdict. It's what God accepts. It's the only thing God accepts. And because God accepts Jesus, He also accepts you. "His divine power has given to us all things that pertain to life and godliness, through the knowledge of Him who has called us to glory and virtue" (2 Peter 1:3).

Lord God, I've broken Your law, and I'm guilty. Your Son is my mediator, and You're my judge. I plead guilty, and Jesus submits the evidence that He already paid the price. You accept my plea of guilt and His declaration as Savior—and with Him, I'm free. Amen.

POWERFUL PRAYER
Truth #72

Prayer is an adventure.

"Ask, and it shall be given to you. Seek, and you shall find. Knock, and it shall be opened to you."

MATTHEW 7:7

Adventure is all about discovery. You might climb a mountain but have no idea of the challenges found between the valley and the summit. Adventure can be thrilling or intimidating; it might pull you from your comfort zone.

If you want directions, you ask. If you are looking for something, you seek. If you want to know if a new life direction is right for you, then you knock on the door of opportunity. These are examples of discovery and are the essence of adventure.

God wants your life to be an adventure. He wants your life to be filled with daily discovery. This life in Christ is not supposed to be a place to sit and grow stale—where boredom sets in and refuses to leave, or where you simply recall adventures from years gone by. No matter your age, you can ask, seek, and knock. You can discover, experience, and take part in new adventures directed by God.

And it starts with prayer.

Ask: Pray to the God who leads all great adventures.
Seek: Read God's Word for the answers you've asked for. (You'll find what you're seeking.)

Knock: Participate in God's great adventure for you.

God will always do the heavy lifting. He will help you when you ask, but the words *ask*, *seek*, and *knock* are all verbs—they signify that you should take action. Adventure will need your cooperation. The opposite view of this verse might be, "Don't ask and have few answers, don't seek and you'll never find, don't knock and you'll discover closed doors."

Let prayer be the start of a spiritual adventure that never needs to end.

Father, the faith You've given me moves beyond a worship
service. It has action, movement, and planning. As I
ask, seek, and knock, help me discover there's more
to this life than a start and an end. Meet me here in
the middle for the adventure of a lifetime. Amen.

POWERFUL PRAYER
Truth #73

Prayer welcomes protection.

[Jesus said,] "I do not ask that You take them out of the world, but that You would keep them from evil."
JOHN 17:15

Becoming and acting like a Christian is a brave choice, and you'll need protection. God doesn't save you only to keep you in a protective bubble. He walks with you and will protect you *as you journey* among those who may be hostile to the God you serve.

Your prayer to God welcomes the protection that Jesus asked God to provide for His followers. This might include protection from Satan, from those who make evil more than a hobby, and even from your own nature that will, from time to time, entertain the desire to break God's laws.

If you want to make a difference in the way God wants you to make a difference, then you will take this prayer and make it a standard request. It's not as if God doesn't know you need protection. It's good that *you* know you need protection—and ask for it. King David understood this truth when he wrote, "Though I walk in the midst of trouble, You will revive me. You shall stretch out Your hand against the wrath of my enemies, and Your right hand shall save me" (Psalm 138:7).

The biggest difference between a Christian and a non-

Christian is not that one struggles and the other doesn't. The primary difference is that one struggles on her own and the other has God to walk with her and offer protection.

God said you would face trouble, but He offers protection from the evil that can damage your heart, wound your spirit, and sear your soul. Pray for that level of protection.

Lord, I need Your protection. That's not just a request; it's an admission that I can't fend off the influence of evil on my own. Help me remember that I'll face difficulty and that Your protection helps me avoid regret-filled choices. That's the protection I need—and You supply. Amen.

POWERFUL PRAYER
Truth #74

Prayer welcomes the Holy Spirit.

*...praying always with all prayer and
supplication in the Spirit, and watching with all
perseverance and supplication for all saints.*

EPHESIANS 6:18

When you pray, you speak to God. You have the ability to pray
because Jesus established a connection with God when He
died to pay the price for your sin. But did you know that the
Holy Spirit is also a major part of prayer?

In John 14:26, Jesus said, "The Comforter, who is the Holy
Spirit, whom the Father will send in My name, He shall teach
you all things and bring to your remembrance all things that
I have said to you."

Your prayers should, at the very least, be influenced by the
Holy Spirit. He teaches, reminds, comforts, guides, and moni-
tors your progress. You can let God's Spirit help you remember
people who could use a prayer, situations that could use God's
help, and decisions that require His wisdom.

It's possible you've only thought about God when praying,
or maybe you've added Jesus to the list of those involved in
your prayer life. However, when you pray with the help of
God's Spirit, you're praying more effectively because you're not
just relying on your mind to come up with the content of your

prayer. You receive God's help—His Holy Spirit—in praying in a way that goes beyond what you'd be able to do on your own.

When you allow God's Spirit to help you, there's another benefit. Paul wrote, "The love of God has been poured out in our hearts by the Holy Spirit who was given to us" (Romans 5:5). God's love is experienced because of His Spirit. And He's always with you.

Father God, I pray to You—in the name of Jesus and with the help of Your Spirit. Sometimes I don't think of the wonder of Your Spirit in helping me pray. May I invite His help every time I talk to You. May I desire to talk to You often. Amen.

POWERFUL PRAYER
Truth #75

Prayer can be birthed in awe.

[Mary said,] And His mercy is on those who
fear Him from generation to generation.

LUKE 1:50

Mary was with child. An angel told her something that had never been spoken before, an idea no one had ever considered, and a rescue plan that was completely unexpected. God's Son would be born into a human family, and Mary, a virgin, would deliver Jesus to the world.

Mary would become the wife of Joseph. The trip to Bethlehem would soon take place. The shepherd's visit would come soon enough. Yet in a time when Mary dreamed of motherhood, she was filled with profound awe.

Before Mary saw Jesus, she worshipped Him. Before she held Him in her arms, she held Him in her heart. Before she saw Him preach His first sermon, she carried good news.

This passage in Luke 1 is often called the Magnificat. It's a passage of awe and wonder over what was coming into the world and the change that would come with Him.

When Mary spoke, she magnified the Lord (verse 46), rejoiced in God (verse 47), admitted God's blessing (verse 48), acknowledged great things God had done (verse 49), called God holy (verse 49), recognized God's mercy (verse 50), and admitted God's strength (verse 51). She saw His acts, including how He rejected pride (verse 51), upheld humility (verse 52), fed the hungry (verse 53), helped His family (verse 54), and never hid Himself from them (verse 55).

This is a quick summary of what Mary's awe looked like. An even shorter version might be "God is stronger, wiser, and more important than me. Yet He loves me and cares for me in ways that bring awe to my heart."

God delights in knowing His gifts can bring you to a place of awe.

Lord, I stand in awe of a risen Savior, a loving God, and the gift of the Spirit. Let this joy overflow the confines of my heart, flood my mind, and spill over my lips for others to hear. Let these words be my personal Magnificat. Amen.

POWERFUL PRAYER
Truth #76

Prayer and praise are companions.

Is anyone among you afflicted? Let him pray.
Is anyone merry? Let him sing psalms.

JAMES 5:13

Life experiences bring different seasons to your prayer life. There will be times of absolute brokenness when you'll cry out to God, asking for the help only He can provide. In these moments, you're certain that if God doesn't show up, then all is lost.

The sons of Korah provided an example of what this sounds like when they wrote, "O LORD God of my salvation, I have cried day and night before You. Let my prayer come before You; incline Your ear to my cry, for my soul is full of troubles, and my life draws near to the grave" (Psalm 88:1–3).

God doesn't flinch or hide from the cry of the desperate. He doesn't stand back and act as if it's no big deal. He doesn't take some kind of pleasure from your pain. When you're afflicted, pray.

There will also be times when inward and outward circumstances are what you'd call "blessed," in which you wear a smile and your heart feels light. Desperation wouldn't describe your experience. When joy overwhelms you, don't forget to worship God in prayer.

King David prayed that kind of prayer in Psalm 145: "I will extol You, my God, O King, and I will bless Your name forever and ever. Every day I will bless You, and I will praise Your name forever and ever. Great is the LORD, and greatly to be praised, and His greatness is unsearchable" (verses 1–3).

God brings His people through times of desperation, so the merging of today's desperation with an understanding of God's goodness can lead the desperate to worship. This truth applies to everyone. It applies to *your* circumstances. In desperation, pray. In anticipation, worship.

God, You're strong enough to handle my desperate moments. I'm weak enough to know I can't. You're wise enough to lead me. Help me be smart enough to follow. And when the day comes when sorrow turns to joy, let ready worship be heard from me to You. Amen.

POWERFUL PRAYER
Truth #77

Prayer requires engagement.

*"But when you pray, do not use vain repetitions
as the heathen do. For they think that they
shall be heard for their many words."*

MATTHEW 6:7

Literature is filled with characters who use spells, incantations, and chants. They believe that if they say the right words in the right order at the right pace—and say them the right number of times—then they'll receive a positive response from some supernatural being.

That's exactly what God wants you to avoid when praying to Him. Prayer is personal, not a performance. God wants to hear your heart, not a recent top-ten list of catchy prayer phrases. Jesus said heathens do that kind of thing. Christians should stop their lips from praying prayers that engage the mouth but do little for the heart.

Why? If prayer becomes a duty, it diminishes effective communication with God.

Think about it this way. Would it be wise for parents to adopt a mechanical approach to talking with their children? Could they say the same ten things every day and expect their children to feel like Mom and Dad really want to know them? Adults might leave the conversation feeling like they are engaged as parents, but the children will think otherwise.

God wants to hear from you, but your prayer can become so automatic that it leaves you unsure if God is listening, and it convinces God that you weren't really engaged in what you were saying. After all, He knows the matters of the heart that have become stuck in your throat—those things that never quite make it into the conversation, and those words that are replaced with vain repetition. Don't let empty words distract you from the real reason you talk to God—relationship.

Dear God, my heart's an open book before You. I can't hide the real me behind words that sound nice but are meaningless. May I engage You in sincere prayer. Help me move my prayers out of neutral and become fully engaged. Amen.

POWERFUL PRAYER
Truth #78

Prayer puts anxiety in its place.

Be anxious for nothing, but in everything,
by prayer and supplication with thanksgiving,
let your requests be made known to God.

PHILIPPIANS 4:6

Watch the news and you'll find a reason to be a pessimist. Situations in this world—even in our own home—can leave a festering claw mark of anxiety.

Worry is normal. It's a response we humans adopt when we feel like things are out of our control. Perhaps the only thing we *do* have some control over is our response to the things we can't control.

When you're filled with worry, sleep will be hard to come by. You might overeat or forget to eat. And it's hard to enjoy the best of days when worry causes you to run down a list of why it's a terrible time to enjoy life. If you're like most people, you buy into worry's argument and agree that God's blessings aren't enough to transform a worried woman into a fear-not follower.

Pray. God's listening, and He'll help lead you away from fear. Need proof? Check out Psalm 34:4: "I sought the LORD, and He heard me and delivered me from all my fears."

God does not want you to live in fear. He wants your life to be defined by love and truth. Need proof? Read 2 Timothy 1:7: "For God has not given us the spirit of fear, but of power and of love and of a sound mind."

God helps you see things clearly and has always been your rescuer. Accept this truth and you don't need to fear anyone. Need proof? Consider Psalm 27:1: "The LORD is my light and my salvation. Whom shall I fear? The LORD is the strength of my life. Of whom shall I be afraid?"

Fear and faith can't coexist. You can't trust God and fear anything else. Which do you choose—trust or fear?

Father God, You're in control. I try to be, but it never ends well. I can't rely on You and still be self-reliant. When I try to do Your job, I fail every time. May my trust in You overcome the worry that wants to be my friend. Amen.

POWERFUL PRAYER
Truth #79

Prayer affirms commitment.

Your word have I hidden in my heart,
that I might not sin against You.

PSALM 119:11

This will be the start of a long look at a biblical prayer. There are 176 verses in Psalm 119; we'll look at twenty-two parts of this prayer. Consider how they work together and discover a few more nuggets of biblical truth to help unlock an improved and powerful prayer life.

God's Word contains wisdom on each page, hope in each story, faith in each book, love in each act of kindness, mercy in each act of God, and answers to life's great questions.

The psalmist admitted God's Word has such value. Commitment to studying the words God placed in His book is implied when you read, "Your word have I hidden in my heart." You can't hide God's Word in the core of who you are if you don't read it or refuse to study.

Why study? "That I might not sin against You." You can break God's law without knowing it. Just because you don't read the Bible doesn't give you an excuse to break God's commands. You can't claim, "I just didn't know."

The Bible exists so you *can* know. You can read it, have it read to you, or listen online. Explore daily Bible reading plans and the many additional study materials that are available.

The more you know about what God wants, the more excuses go away. . .and faith can begin to take action. You'll have a good handle on how to obey because you'll discover God's plan.

Give God a place where He can store His Word in your life for easy retrieval. Following Him requires obedience. Obedience needs instruction. Instruction comes from His Word.

Lord, Your Word gives instruction. It defines
Your wise choices for humankind. When I fail to
learn what it says, I can't become more like You.
The best I can hope for is a kinder me. As I pray,
may I be committed to hearing from You. Amen.

POWERFUL PRAYER
Truth # 80

Prayer counts blessings.

I have rejoiced in the way of Your
testimonies, as much as in all riches.
PSALM 119:14

The finest home can't compare. The most prestigious job pales in comparison. The highest fashion, fastest car, and most expensive toys seem meaningless. You could have all the money in the world and still not be as rich as you are with the blessings of God. The apostle Paul wrote in Philippians 3:8–10, "I count all things but loss for the excellency of the knowledge of Christ Jesus my Lord, for whom I have suffered the loss of all things and count them but dung, that I may win Christ and be found in Him, not having my own righteousness, which is of the law, but that which is through the faith of Christ, the righteousness that is of God by faith, that I may know Him and the power of His resurrection and the fellowship of His sufferings, being made conformable to His death."

We get to pursue what is most meaningful to us in life. Some choose things, some choose fame, some choose people, but the wisest among us choose God. His blessings make things meaningless, fame fleeting, people a reflection of His love, and God the primary focal point.

Perhaps God's greatest blessing is wisdom. It starts with

recognizing that He can and will rescue you, but it extends the offer to understand who He is, how to please Him, and where to turn for help. You may not have thought of these things as blessings because there's no monetary value attached to these gifts, but consider this: "For what shall it profit a man if he gains the whole world and loses his own soul?" (Mark 8:36).

Rejoice that God's blessings are priceless.

Lord God, I admit there are times I only think of blessings as an easy life and no financial stress. I think of tangible gifts—things I can touch, feel, and possess. Help me to remember that knowing You and learning from You are among Your greatest blessings. Amen.

POWERFUL PRAYER
Truth #81

Prayer asks for wisdom.

*Open my eyes, that I may see wondrous
things from Your law.*
PSALM 119:18

It's possible you've tried to read the Bible and came away more confused than before you started. The Bible is God's Word and contains things you need to know in order to live a life that pleases God. But you'll need to ask God to open your eyes to see and understand His truth.

This isn't a request for your physical eyes to focus on the words of a page, but for improved vision for your spiritual eyes so the core of who you are can begin to examine truth, understand it, and find ways to apply it to daily choices.

Paul wrote, "But the natural man does not receive the things of the Spirit of God, for they are foolishness to him. Nor can he know them, because they are spiritually discerned" (1 Corinthians 2:14). Before becoming a Christian, you were considered a natural woman. God was an abstract idea or just part of family tradition. You may have felt it was impossible to break God's law if there was no God. You couldn't be accountable if you didn't believe. The idea of believing in a being you've never seen seemed foolish. You may have thought you were the rational one and Christians were crazy. Hebrews 11:1 explains what Christians know and natural people have yet to learn: "Now faith is the substance of things hoped for, the evidence of things not seen."

Faith comes first, followed by improved spiritual vision. *Then* you can begin to discern the truth that starts in Genesis and is located in every book of the Bible.

God, I want the wisdom only You can give. I want
understanding so I can put wisdom in perspective.
I want to discern those things that help me
understand You better. May faith convince my mind,
and may I see life as You intended it. Amen.

POWERFUL PRAYER
Truth #82

Prayer acknowledges injustice.

Princes also sat and spoke against me,
but Your servant meditated on Your statutes.

PSALM 119:23

Gossip, lies, and misinformation are found everywhere—the coffee shop, truck stop, grocery store, and even church. God calls it sin, and this God-law is broken frequently.

The psalmist reported that princes spoke against him, likely behind his back and in front of strangers. We still see that today. People who should know better tell stories that are not firsthand accounts, and they damage reputations. They heard from someone who heard from someone that someone else did something. This information is shared as a matter of concern or for prayer. However, the person who tells the story and the one who hears it have no way to verify the story unless they talk directly to the person being discussed, which rarely happens. For the psalmist, this slanderous conversation was considered an injustice. By God's standard, the psalmist was right.

In the book of Proverbs we read, "He who goes about as a talebearer reveals secrets; therefore, do not meddle with him who flatters with his lips" (Proverbs 20:19).

People who gossip make it seem as if they're doing you a favor by sharing information. They can make you feel like a privileged insider who is worthy of receiving classified information. God wants you to walk away from these less-than-affirming encounters.

Recognize the injustice for what it is. Pray for God's intervention. And then get into God's Word and explore the many options God offers that will ultimately mean time better spent. God's laws always draw you closer to Him and further away from those who speak against you or others. Spending time with God will positively impact your relationships, reactions, and responses.

Father, keep my voice from sharing stories about people when I don't know if the information is accurate and when I haven't talked to them first. Help me recognize injustice, pray for those involved, and refresh my perspective by reading Your Word. Amen.

POWERFUL PRAYER
Truth #83

Prayer prepares you to share.

*Make me to understand the way of Your precepts,
so I shall tell of Your wondrous works.*

PSALM 119:27

When you buy a house, you share the news. When your child makes the honor roll, you buy a bumper sticker that says so. When you win an award, you post it on social media. It's natural to share good news. Yet it's possible to have access to the best news humankind will ever know and never share it.

The psalmist didn't want to treat God's story as a secret. This led him to pray for more understanding. Many times, a lack of understanding keeps us silent. We don't want to sound like we don't know what we're talking about. . .so we don't talk at all. Words God could use to point someone to Him remain unsaid. People who need to know this best news are left to wonder if it really exists.

In John 14:21 Jesus said, "He who has My commandments and keeps them, it is he who loves Me. And he who loves Me shall be loved by My Father, and I will love him, and will reveal Myself to him." When you learn more, God entrusts more. When you obey more, you show love more. When you understand more, you can share more. Your prayer life can prepare you for more because you can ask God to help you share what you actually know.

Jesus made this promise in John 8:31–32: "If you continue in My word, then you are My disciples indeed. And you shall know the truth, and the truth shall make you free."

There's freedom in following Christ. There's freedom in knowing the truth. There's freedom in praying that God would help you share *more*.

Dear God, I want more of You so I can share more of You. I don't want to be in the dark when it comes to knowing You. I want to be a light for You to people who need an introduction. I want You to be priority one. Amen.

POWERFUL PRAYER
Truth #84

Prayer asks for strength.

My soul melts for heaviness.
Strengthen me according to Your word.
PSALM 119:28

Too many life-altering events arriving close together can lead to depression. This might include a health crisis, the loss of a loved one, a job change, or significant issues with a child. One blow after another can make it much harder to bounce back. External and internal pressures build. The psalmist said this could leave you with a heavy, melted soul.

This feeling may be something you identify with. King David was certainly familiar with it. He wrote, "Give ear to my prayer, O God, and do not hide Yourself from my supplication. . . . My heart is greatly pained within me" (Psalm 55:1, 4). David needed strength, and every source he knew to draw from was out of stock—except one. A prayer to God means access to strength that exceeds your own and goes beyond that of anyone who steps in to help. While you need the help of friends when trouble visits, the source of strength that pulls you out of a rut and away from the brink is found in God alone.

God made sure there's an abundance of encouragement in His Word. Imagine feeling desperate and weak and coming across these verses: "'My grace is sufficient for you, for My strength is made perfect in weakness.' Therefore, I will boast most gladly even more in my weaknesses, that the power of Christ may rest on me. Therefore I take pleasure in weaknesses, in reproaches, in necessities, in persecutions, in distresses, for Christ's sake. For when I am weak, then I am strong" (2 Corinthians 12:9–10).

You're not alone, you've never been alone, and you'll never be alone. Pray when you're down. Look up and find strength. God can make your heavy heart light.

Father, when I'm downcast and I have a heavy, melted soul, let me take the fragments of pain and give them to You. Help me make them a gift so You can make something new. And while You're rebuilding, may I be grateful for Your personal encouragement. Amen.

POWERFUL PRAYER
Truth #85

Prayer acknowledges the need for mercy.

Let Your mercies come also to me, O Lord,
even Your salvation, according to Your word.
PSALM 119:41

Mercy is a verdict releasing you from discipline for an offense, although there may still be consequences. When people throw themselves at the mercy of the court, they're asking for a lighter sentence. God is a God of justice, but His mercy is evidence of His willingness to forgive. Sometimes mercy looks a bit like salvation—it's undeserved but a gracious gift beyond expectation.

The psalmist could invite God's mercy because God's Word described Him as merciful.

In Luke 6:36 Jesus said, "Therefore you be merciful, as your Father also is merciful." Luke 6:35 fills in the "therefore" details: "But love your enemies, and do good, and lend, hoping for nothing back. And your reward shall be great, and you shall be the children of the Highest. For He is kind to the unthankful and to the evil."

There's a lot to consider in this verse. You should love those you consider enemies because God loved you when you were His enemy. God is kind to people who are ungrateful and evil. So, when you pray for God's mercy, you need to live the lifestyle of the merciful.

James wrote, "He who has shown no mercy shall have judgment without mercy; and mercy rejoices over judgment" (James 2:13). Rejoice when God offers you mercy. Rejoice when God offers mercy to others. If God can show mercy to you, don't demand that He only show justice to others.

Instead, show mercy because you've been shown mercy. Love your enemies because you were once God's enemy. Aren't you glad some things change?

Lord God, You want to identify injustice. You even want me to stand up for those who've been a victim of injustice. You don't want me to accept Your mercy and never show it to others. Help me to be merciful. Amen.

POWERFUL PRAYER
Truth #86

Prayer is an immediate connection.

*At midnight I will rise to give thanks to You
because of Your righteous judgments.*

PSALM 119:62

What time did the psalmist rise to give thanks to God? Did he have to wait until traditional business hours? Did he have to make sure it wasn't God's break time? *No.* The psalmist rose in the middle of the night and expressed gratitude. He was neither early nor late. Midnight was a perfect time to talk to God. So is 2:32 a.m., 4:44 p.m., or 10:15 p.m.

There's no wrong time to pray. Your prayers don't need to wait. You have an immediate connection to God in moments when sleep has bolted past your bedroom door and left you needing to talk things over. Maybe these times are unexpected appointments to pray. The psalmist said, "My help comes from the LORD, who made heaven and earth. He will not allow your foot to be moved; He who keeps you will not slumber" (Psalm 121:2–3).

God keeps watch over you always. He is ready to listen to you anytime. He offers rescue—even in the middle of the night. He doesn't nod off, get drowsy, or put your prayers on SILENT. When you pray, you're heard. From the moment you mention His name, God is listening. When you don't know what to say, God understands.

Still not convinced? Read Psalm 55:16–17: "I will call on God, and the LORD shall save me. Evening and morning and at noon I will pray and cry aloud, and He shall hear my voice." This should encourage the most timid of souls. You don't have to beg, set an appointment, or wonder if it's a bad time to call on God. You don't have to try to figure things out before asking for help either. When you need wisdom, ask. Prayer is always available on demand.

Lord God, I don't need to pay attention to the time when I pray. When I need to talk, You're ready to listen. When I have problems, You have solutions. When I wake in fear, help me remember that the darkest night can't stand before Your light. Amen.

POWERFUL PRAYER
Truth #87

Prayer makes believers friends.

*I am a companion of all those who fear You
and of those who keep Your precepts.*

PSALM 119:63

The psalmist said he was friends with a certain type of person—one who follows God and obeys His commands. Christian friendships are so important for believers, and it doesn't matter how long you've been a Christian. Both newbies and veterans in the faith can gain from the companionship of fellow believers. We walk with younger Christians to encourage *their* faith. We walk with mature Christians to encourage *our* faith. And in both cases, we encourage each other's faith.

In Ecclesiastes 4:9–10 Solomon explained a very practical reason for the companionship of the faithful: "Two are better than one, because they have a good reward for their labor. For if they fall, the one will lift up his companion, but woe to him who is alone when he falls, for he does not have another to help him up."

When it comes to your faith walk, two are always better than one. God can—and will—use other Christians to help you grow. God invites you to pray with other Christians too. Praying with others is a vulnerable act because it can expose some of your insecurities, but it's also a way to learn to care more about others while everyone draws close to the God who hears and answers prayer.

Proverbs 17:9 adds some additional advice on the subject of companionship: "He who covers a transgression seeks love, but he who repeats a matter separates friends." If you learn something about someone when you pray with that person, don't repeat it like common gossip. You'll betray a trust and jeopardize a friendship.

Prayer with friends is a profound blessing. It provides mutual encouragement and promotes the value of Christian family.

Father, Your Son, Jesus, had friends on earth. He prayed with them, and they learned from Him. Help me welcome the opportunity to pray for and with other Christians. I'll need their friendship and could use their encouragement. These are friendships that You inspired. Thanks. Amen.

POWERFUL PRAYER
Truth #88

Prayer acknowledges lessons learned.

Before I was afflicted I went astray,
but now I have kept Your word.

PSALM 119:67

You probably aren't on a global search for perfect Christians.
You can look at your own life and conclude that finding a perfect Christian would be like locating a unicorn. And if you do
find a self-proclaimed perfect Christian, you really wouldn't
believe her. Maybe that's because there was only one human
being who was perfect: Jesus. The writer of Hebrews said, "For
we do not have a high priest who cannot be concerned with
the feeling of our weaknesses, but was in all points tempted
as we are, yet without sin" (Hebrews 4:15).

Jesus was tempted. He didn't sin. You are tempted, but sin
is a common outcome.

Yet prayer not only admits that God's right and you've been
wrong but also acknowledges that you are learning lessons.
Good is being developed in your life even in the middle of
wayward moments. This can't happen if you make a habit of
going astray and stiff-arming God's discipline to bring you
back. It happens when you turn away from the choice to sin
and toward the God who forgives.

God never wants you to sin so you somehow become more

relatable to others. He wants you to obey, admit it's hard, and acknowledge that failure is common.

Christians who act like they're perfect usually aren't believed—or their facade just amplifies feelings of failure among others who admit they aren't perfect. This is your story: you sin, God disciplines, then you follow Him once more. Every part of that universal story can be shared. Tell your story and share it honestly. People will accept it much more than false perfection.

God, I'm a sinner who has been rescued by Your grace. Everything about salvation is a gift from You. Being a Christian doesn't mean I'll never fail. It means there's a place I can come back to when I fail. You're teaching; I'm learning. Keep me on track. Amen.

POWERFUL PRAYER
Truth #89

Prayer acknowledges God as a personal Creator.

Your hands have made me and fashioned me.

PSALM 119:73

God personally created you.

And that's not all. God made air to breathe, food to eat, and water to drink. He cared enough about you to create everything required for you to live—trees to make a home, seeds to grow crops, and the sun to make those things grow. God didn't leave anything out. If you needed it, God created it. Then He made things you didn't need but would please you, like waterfalls, mountains, and stars.

God created the first man, Adam, from the dust of the ground (Genesis 2:7). Solomon made it clear that this is the condition of all men. In Ecclesiastes 3:20 he wrote, "All go to one place; all are of the dust, and all turn to dust again."

Before God made man, He made dust. He took the very thing you wash from your hands and used it to make everything else. What you sweep from a mudroom floor, God uses to create life. It starts as dust, ends as dust, and in that time in between, you get to discover the God who made the dust—the God who made you.

Maybe God used the common—the dust under your feet—to

remind you that His future for you is uncommon. Paul wrote, "For we who are in this tabernacle groan, being burdened—not that we would be unclothed, but clothed, that mortality might be swallowed up by life" (2 Corinthians 5:4).

You may have started as dust, but God has better things planned for your future. He created you to experience heaven.

Father God, if You took such amazing care to create me from dust, I can't imagine what my new body in heaven will be like. You give good gifts; help me to be a good receiver. You're an amazing Creator; help me to be a grateful creation. Amen.

POWERFUL PRAYER
Truth # 90

Prayer expresses hope.

I hope in Your word.
PSALM 119:81

You can hope for a better job, house, or income. You can hope fame or prestige finds you. You can even hope that tomorrow is better than today, that your children have a better future, or that your car lasts a little longer. But this is a different hope than you'll find in the Bible.

In most cases, when the Bible uses the word *hope,* it's not just wishful thinking. Hope is assurance, trust, and belief that something is true, even before it's seen. It's a close cousin to faith. The evidence is found in Romans 8:24–25: "For we are saved in hope, but hope that is seen is not hope. For why does a man still hope for what he sees? But if we hope for what we do not see, then we wait for it with patience."

Prayer expresses hope. It recalls the things God promised that you're looking forward to. It recalls things that have happened, in part, but have not been fully realized. It looks forward to meeting God face to face. Paul desired this for believers: "Now may the God of hope fill you with all joy and peace in believing, that you may abound in hope through the power of the Holy Spirit" (Romans 15:13).

The Bible describes hope as your soul's anchor. Hope holds

you fast to what you need the most. It keeps Jesus as your primary focus. It promises a future inheritance with God: "That being justified by His grace, we should be made heirs according to the hope of eternal life" (Titus 3:7).

There is no wishful thinking involved in eternal life. It is promised, assured, and evidenced by faithful hope.

Lord God, my hope in You can be sure by believing that what You said You'll do. My prayers express hope. This hope doesn't leave me to wonder. Help me trust Your Word, heart, and promises. One day, they'll lead me home. Amen.

POWERFUL PRAYER
Truth #91

Prayer admits that God is truth.

Forever, O LORD, Your word is settled in heaven.
PSALM 119:89

God never sent an angel to tell someone something He didn't mean. God never plays jokes on humankind. God never does anything to betray the trust of those who believe.

This is important because if God ever proved unworthy of trust, then it would be difficult—if not impossible—for you to believe He's entirely loving, long-sufferingly patient, and forever faithful. Let this soak in. God will never make fun of you. When He speaks to you, His words are said as a forever truth. He doesn't change His mind. His "word is settled in heaven."

Just because you may be used to people letting you down, going back on their word, and withholding truth, never assume that God has any interest in doing the same. This is something God cannot do. Paul wrote, "If we do not believe, still He remains faithful. He cannot deny Himself" (2 Timothy 2:13). God *cannot be*, *will not be*, and *never has been* unfaithful.

You'll experience more power in your prayer life when you're convinced that God is the only source of truth. Jesus affirmed this when He prayed for those who followed Him, "Sanctify them through Your truth. Your word is truth" (John 17:17). To sanctify means to make holy. . .to make holy means to be set apart for a good purpose. . .to be set apart means to think differently. . .to think differently means a change in actions. God's truth found in His Word makes this chain reaction possible.

God's truth is settled in the heavens. . .and it's available to you—right now.

Lord, it would be hard to believe You if anything You said was untrue. It would be foolish to trust You if You said one thing and did another. Thank You for being committed to truth. It just makes sense for me to trust the truth of Your Word. Amen.

POWERFUL PRAYER
Truth #92

Prayer admits that God speaks through His Word.

How sweet are Your words to my taste!
Yes, sweeter than honey to my mouth!
PSALM 119:103

Did you know that God wants you to have a sweet tooth? No, not the sugar kind—the scripture kind. The Bible can become as desirable as your favorite snack, and it's much healthier. The psalmist said, "O taste and see that the LORD is good. Blessed is the man who trusts in Him" (Psalm 34:8).

If God's Word is a food basket, there's no better assortment of perfect tastes. Peter told believers, "Laying aside all malice, and all deceit, and hypocrisies, and envies, and all evil speakings, as newborn babies, desire the sincere milk of the word, that you may grow by it, if indeed you have tasted that the Lord is gracious" (1 Peter 2:1–3).

Babies always accept new things into their world by tasting them. If they want to know more about something, they taste it. In a spiritual sense, you're encouraged to do this with God's Word. Take God's Word internally and see that it's perfectly suited to help you grow, to explain how to interact with God.

God made the figurative literal when He spoke to the prophet Ezekiel: "'Son of man, cause your belly to eat, and fill your body with this scroll that I give you.' Then I ate it, and it was as honey for sweetness in my mouth" (Ezekiel 3:3).

When was the last time you told God that His Word was sweet and satisfying to your soul?

God speaks through the Bible. When you accept what He says, expect it to satisfy your spiritual hunger.

Father God, sometimes I'm spiritually starved. Sometimes I fill up on useless snacks that never satisfy and leave me with little room to feed on Your Word. Give me an appetite for Your Word. Remind me: this is the way You speak. Let me taste. Let me be satisfied. Amen.

POWERFUL PRAYER
Truth #93

Prayer admits that God's Word makes things clear.

Your word is a lamp to my feet and a light to my path.
PSALM 119:105

Imagine being dropped off in a country field in the dark of night. You have the moon and stars, but neither is bright enough to clearly point the way from where you are to where you want to be. It feels a little unsafe, and you might experience a good bit of fear.

The quick answer to your dilemma is to try a flashlight. It doesn't completely erase the dark, but it lights enough space in front of you so you don't fall when taking your next step.

God often gives you just enough light into your future to help you take one more step, and then another. Sometimes you only get one answer at a time. Sometimes you wish sunrise would come so you could see what seems so fearful in the dark.

You might even find someone approaching in your spiritual darkness and offering directions. The apostle John provided some advice on how to deal with this spiritual issue: test the source! "Beloved, do not believe every spirit, but test the spirits, whether they are of God, because many false prophets have gone out into the world. By this you know the Spirit of God: every spirit that confesses that Jesus Christ has come in the flesh is of God, and every spirit that does not confess that Jesus Christ has come in the flesh is not of God" (1 John 4:1–3).

Darkness is frightening, but God makes your way clear enough to keep walking; and when the dawn rises, you can see clearly that God led you to a better place. This would be the perfect time to pray and thank Him for the direction He offers when darkness is crushing.

Dear God, when I'm immersed in the unknown, help me seek Your light and use it to follow Your path. When I stumble, help me to remember that Your light is found in Your Word. If I don't read it, I don't see Your plan. Make things clear to me as I read Your Word. Amen.

POWERFUL PRAYER
Truth #94

Prayer expresses gratitude for refuge.

*You are my hiding place and my
shield; I hope in Your word.*
PSALM 119:114

The manufacturer of a bath product once claimed that it would take you away from the struggles you faced. An airline company suggested that when you messed up and needed to get away, they were the right airline for you. Owners of vacation destinations want you to know they offer the restorative touch you need.

The psalmist knew that when he faced struggles, messed up, or needed to be restored, God was his first and best choice. He admitted this truth and expressed it in prayer. His example is your example.

God is your hiding place—your refuge, which means you can trust Him and be completely honest (Psalm 62:8), expect His help (Psalm 32:7), find no reason for fear (Psalm 46:1–2), and discover safety (Proverbs 18:10).

Even when you're tempted to do the wrong thing, you can look to God as a refuge. Paul wrote, "No temptation has taken you but such as is common to man. But God is faithful, who will not allow you to be tempted above what you are able, but with the temptation will also make a way of escape, that you may be able to bear it" (1 Corinthians 10:13).

God makes His love for you clear. He is a refuge and fortress and has very strong arms to rescue you. This is the encouragement you need. You don't have to look for it on social media or in pithy quotes. Israel's most famous king illustrated both the need for encouragement and where to find it; when distressed, "David encouraged himself in the LORD his God" (1 Samuel 30:6).

Turn to your refuge. Pray to the God of encouragement.

Father God, You are what I need. You are trustworthy and want to help me. In You, I'm safe. In You, I'm secure. And only You can take my fear and give me faith in exchange. Thanks for the encouragement You send every time I read Your Word. Amen.

POWERFUL PRAYER
Truth # 95

Prayer invites God to speak.

Uphold me according to Your word, that I may live.
PSALM 119:116

Lots of kids over the years have said, "My dad is stronger than your dad." When you say that about your heavenly Father, there is *no one* who can ever prove you wrong. God is stronger than anyone and anything.

God spoke and the world was created. We see it in Genesis; the psalmist also spoke of God's power when he wrote, "For He spoke, and it was done. He commanded, and it stood fast" (Psalm 33:9).

God has never had trouble with words. What He says has meaning. God's strength is promised by His Word; expect it. Paul said of Jesus, "For by Him all things were created that are in heaven and that are on earth, visible and invisible, whether they are thrones or dominions or principalities or powers. All things were created by Him and for Him" (Colossians 1:16). Things happen when God speaks.

If God can create by simply speaking, then He can sustain, uphold, and help you. What prevents you from asking? God's Word encourages us to "come boldly to the throne of grace, that we may obtain mercy and find grace to help in time of need" (Hebrews 4:16).

God's grace is enough to handle any trouble you face. His Word is powerful enough to offer instruction, wisdom, and assistance. His actions are enough to prove His love for you. God has always been *enough*.

Pray for God's Word to reach your mind, fill your heart, and affect your speech. Pray to the God of words because they have always brought life, love, and light. The God who upholds has been waiting to hear from you.

Lord, Your Word is powerful and perfect. Your Word is truth without deception. Your Word is hope without a single broken promise. I can trust You with my life, love You through my obedience, and follow You with a grateful heart. Speak. I'm listening. Amen.

POWERFUL PRAYER
Truth #96

Prayer invites God to plan your way.

*Order my steps in Your word, and do not let
any iniquity have dominion over me.*

PSALM 119:133

People follow their car's navigation system and sometimes wind up in the middle of a field or near the edge of a cliff. The end result doesn't match their intended destination. They knew where they wanted to go, but technology took them somewhere else.

God can also take you somewhere you hadn't planned, but He promised the following: "A man's heart devises his way, but the LORD directs his steps" (Proverbs 16:9). You can set a goal, make a plan, or devise your way, but God has always had veto power. He'll give you a better set of directions to follow. The end destination will always be better than your original plan.

If you know God can and *wants* to help you, why not pray with the psalmist, "Order my steps in Your word"? When it comes to God's steps or a bad plan, it's a difference between holiness (being set apart for a good purpose) and iniquity (a choice where sin thrives). Jesus told His disciples to follow Him (Matthew 4:19). God told Jonah to go to Nineveh (Jonah 1:2). The disciples followed and were blessed. Jonah didn't want to follow and spent time learning to pray inside a big fish.

If you're looking for a blessing instead of a time-out, hope can be found in Psalm 1:1–2. "Blessed is the man who does not walk in the counsel of the ungodly or stand in the way of sinners or sit in the seat of the scornful. But his delight is in the law of the LORD, and on His law he meditates day and night."

There's safety and protection in God's ordered steps. There's no good time not to follow.

Dear God, I don't want to demand things my way, but I'll make that mistake. I don't want to ignore You, but I probably will. I don't want to miss Your directions, but I might not be paying attention. Guide me and help me pay attention. Amen.

POWERFUL PRAYER
Truth # 97

Prayer weeps for sinners.

Rivers of waters run down my eyes,
because they do not keep Your law.
PSALM 119:136

Once you taste and see that the Lord is good and find joy in following God's footsteps, you may discover heartbreak for other people.

Jeremiah is thought of as "the weeping prophet" because he knew what it meant to follow God when most people wanted nothing to do with Him. He knew what it was like to plead with people to change their minds and have those people make fun of, disregard, or ridicule him. Jeremiah wept for lost people.

The psalmist did the same thing. He wrote that he shed rivers of water because people were bent on rebellion instead of obedience, lawlessness instead of godliness, and destruction instead of discipleship.

Today's verse in Psalm 119 isn't an isolated incident of a psalmist with tears shed over the rebellious. In Psalm 42:3 the psalmist wrote, "My tears have been my food day and night, while they continually say to me, 'Where is your God?'"

Where is God? With us—and for us. "'For I know the thoughts that I think toward you,' says the LORD, 'thoughts of peace and not of evil, to give you an expected end'" (Jeremiah

29:11). It's hard to read something like Jeremiah wrote and not feel broken for those who follow their own path. God's declaration is great news for believers, but the prophet would watch people utterly reject the God who made such a kind offer.

Wouldn't it be nice if you could just make people love Jesus? Maybe, but then they would miss out on a discovery that's wonderful because it's personal. Pray for the lawless, weep over them—and allow God to turn rebellion into rescue.

Father, Your Son wept over Jerusalem, just like Jeremiah wept for his people and the psalmist felt sorrow for the ungodly. Give me a heart that cares that deeply about people who need to find You. May my prayers connect with Your heart about people You love. Amen.

POWERFUL PRAYER
Truth # 98

Prayer acknowledges the righteousness of God.

Your righteousness is an everlasting righteousness, and Your law is the truth.
PSALM 119:142

Sometimes a teacher has a favorite student. Sometimes a boss has a favorite employee. Sometimes a grandparent has a favorite grandchild.

But God never plays favorites. His love for you is absolute and is neither more nor less than His love for anyone else in the world. You can't make Him love you more and He won't love you less.

God made a covenant—or pact—with His family when Jesus died. He paid the penalty for the lawless acts of humankind. This is a binding contract defining how God interacts with you and what you can expect from Him. The psalmist understood that the righteousness of God never ends, never fails, and is never overlooked.

God wants you to be righteous and abide by the terms of His covenant with you. When Jesus saw the Pharisees and their outward display of "holier than thou," He said to His followers, "For I say to you, that unless your righteousness exceeds the righteousness of the scribes and Pharisees, you shall in no circumstance enter into the kingdom of heaven" (Matthew 5:20). Jesus was serious about the difference between cleaning up well and having a heart sold out to God.

Yes, God is righteous, and He wants you to be righteous. This isn't a part-time faith for part-time Christians who are only willing to follow part-time. This is life-changing, destination-altering, and heart-rearranging faith. The apostle Paul told Timothy, "Follow righteousness, faith, love, peace with those who call on the Lord out of a pure heart" (2 Timothy 2:22).

Christians follow a God who's kept His promises even when they've broken the terms of the contract. Remember, His love is given independent of your faithfulness. Still, pursue righteousness.

Lord, You're righteous and call me to be righteous. To act righteous without being righteous is to be a hypocrite. I will fail. Help me admit it when I do. You are right. Help me follow Your directions. You want to change my heart. May I always let You make changes. Amen.

POWERFUL PRAYER
Truth #99

Prayer admits the existence of spiritual treasure.

I rejoice at Your word, as one who finds great plunder.
PSALM 119:162

Forrest Fenn was an art dealer and just quirky enough to make a name for himself beyond his death. Fenn wrote a poem that's included in his memoirs. The poem has attracted attention because it's said to lead to a treasure somewhere in the Rocky Mountains. Fenn's idea was that if someone took the time to read and learn from his poem, they could find his treasure. As of this writing, no one has.

You have the opportunity to find great treasure. All it takes is a willingness to read. And God's Word will have infinitely more value than the elusive treasure of Forrest Fenn.

Jesus said, "Do not lay up for yourselves treasures on earth, where moth and rust corrupt, and where thieves break in and steal. But lay up for yourselves treasures in heaven, where neither moth nor rust corrupts, and where thieves do not break in or steal. For where your treasure is, there your heart will be also" (Matthew 6:19–21).

Hide your treasure in a mountain cave and it may be reclaimed by time and decay, but the treasure found in God's Word is vibrant, real, "living and powerful and sharper than any two-edged sword. . .a discerner of the thoughts and intentions of the heart" (Hebrews 4:12).

Your greatest treasure on earth is what you can read in God's Word. Your greatest treasure in heaven is being forever in God's presence. Both treasures come from what you learn from a spiritual treasure map called the Bible. It's not a treasure that only one person can find. Everyone who seeks can find it (see Matthew 7:8). Pray for God's wisdom. He'll lead you to real treasure.

Dear God, transform my thinking. Help me read Your Word as a map that is equipping me for a profound treasure adventure. Sometimes reading can seem like a duty, something to check off a list of things to do, but You have treasure. Help me discover it in the Bible. Amen.

POWERFUL PRAYER
Truth #100

Prayer admits being lost.

I have gone astray like a lost sheep; seek Your servant.
PSALM 119:176

"I once was lost but now am found." You've probably sung those words before. The lyric is a very simple and precise description of what it's like before meeting Jesus and what it's like after meeting Jesus. Lost, then found.

Jesus may have thought about Psalm 119:176 when He told a parable that began with a question: "What man of you, having a hundred sheep, if he loses one of them, does not leave the ninety-nine in the wilderness and go after what is lost until he finds it?" (Luke 15:4). Lost, then found. Adding to the weight of evidence, Isaiah wrote, "We all like sheep have gone astray. We have turned, each one, to his own way" (Isaiah 53:6). Lost, and the need to be found.

"Was blind but now I see." You didn't know where to look, so God sought you. Prayer is an admission that you're lost. It's a request for directions. It's joy over being found. Invite God to find you. Admit you're far from the God who left the ninety-nine to look for you.

"How precious did that grace appear the hour I first believed." God is in the business of finding lost sheep. He seeks those who go astray. Consider it precious when His grace impacts your need.

"Grace will lead me home." When this life ends and eternity stretches out before you, it's probable you'll remember the moment you were found. The moment you believed. The moment you discovered treasure in God's Word. Heaven is a place of praise because it will be 100 percent filled with people who were lost, then found.

Is it any wonder it's called *amazing* grace?

Lord, I'd still be lost if it weren't for You. The grace You offer is more than I could expect and beyond my understanding. I follow You because You found me. I learn from You because You're my treasure. Keep teaching. I'll keep learning. Amen.

POWERFUL PRAYER
Truth #101

Prayer longs for Jesus' return.

Even so, come, Lord Jesus.
REVELATION 22:20

This prayer journey is nearly at an end. You've discovered ways to interact with God in prayer, things to recognize and admit when praying, and why prayer connects you with the God who gives life to all living things. You've learned the power of encouragement and the need for wisdom and help only God can provide. Prayer advice came from the Old and New Testaments. And each bit of wisdom was sparked inside God's treasure book and brought to these pages.

Perhaps it's fitting to make the final entry in this book of Bible truths the final prayer found in the Bible. This prayer was uttered by John in the book of Revelation. John was an older man when he wrote the book. He'd seen much in his life. All the other disciples had been martyred; he'd been exiled, and he was likely weary. But this apostle had also just witnessed a vision of things that would happen in the end times. He saw things he couldn't understand but were clearly devastating. In this bleak set of circumstances, John prayed, "Even so, come, Lord Jesus."

The longing for God's will and eternity with Him should outpace an interest in your temporary home. God describes this life as mist, vapor, or fire—nothing lasting very long. The apostle Paul identified with John when he wrote, "For our citizenship is in heaven, from where we also look for the Savior, the Lord Jesus Christ" (Philippians 3:20).

Jesus has plans for a new era in your relationship with Him in heaven. After all you've learned and after all you've lived through, praying for the return of Jesus may mean you're making a decision to follow God until He leads home.

Dear Lord, may I never be so tied to this world that I would resent Your Son's return. May I look forward to heaven while appreciating the world You've made for me to enjoy. Heaven should never be something to dread but worth the wait until Jesus returns. Amen.

ANOTHER GREAT RESOURCE FOR WOMEN

There's no greater personality than Jesus—so why not make time each day to know Him better? This 365-day devotional highlights aspects of Jesus' life and work, His teaching and impact on women's lives, in inspirational pieces providing food for thought each morning—and an inspiring prayer for bedtime.

Hardcover / 978-1-63609-720-6

Find This and More from Barbour Publishing at Your Favorite Bookstore or www.barbourbooks.com